Building Time

The Center for Basque Studies
Occasional Papers Series, No. 22

Building Time

The Relatus in Frank Gehry's Architecture

Iñaki Begiristain Mitxelena

Translated by Sarah J. Turtle and
Iñaki Mendiguren

Center for Basque Studies
University of Nevada, Reno

The book was published with the generaous financial assistance of the Basque Government.

Occasional Papers Series, No. 22
Series Editors: Joseba Zulaika and Cameron J. Watson

Center for Basque Studies
University of Nevada, Reno
Reno, Nevada 89557
http://basque.unr.edu

Book design: Kimberly Daggett
Cover photo: Iñaki Begiristain Mitxelena

Library of Congress Cataloging-in-Publication Data

Begiristain Mitxelena, Iñaki, 1964- author.
[Fikzioak eta relatus berrien eraikuntza. English]
Building Time : the relatus in Gehry's architecture / Iñaki Begiristain Mitxelena ; translated by Sarah J. Turtle and Iñaki Mendiguren.
pages cm. -- (Occasional papers series ; no. 22)
Includes bibliographical references and index.
ISBN 978-1-935709-50-3 (pbk. : alk. paper)
1. Gehry, Frank O., 1929---Criticism and interpretation. 2. Architecture--California--Los Angeles Region--History--20th century. 3. Architecture--Philosophy. I. Title.

NA737.G44B47 2014
720.92--dc23

2014002985

Ithaca gave you the delightful voyage.

—Constantine P. Cavafy, "Ithaca"

Contents

Acknowledgments

I want to express my gratitude to the following friends and colleagues for their help:

Juhani Pallasmaa, for the attention that he has lent to this work and for his energy. My colleagues Iñigo Garcia Odiaga, Ibon Salaberria, Javier Puldain and Santos Bregaña for their critical reading and rich contributions. In Los Angeles, Annie Katata, Eric Randolph, Martin Casteran, Tom Hoos, and Pavel Getov for their hospitality and help. To Ed Mastro and Andres Carrillo from the Cabrillo Marine Aquarium and Trevor Belden at Edgemar for the valuable interviews and information. Joseba Zulaika for accepting to serve as the director of this work. Iñaki Mendiguren and Sarah Turtle, for their Basque to English translation. Daniel Montero, from the Center for Basque Studies, for his patience in the book's preparation and publication.

And, especially, my wife Amaia, and our children Inge, Lander, and Arrate, for their confidence in me, help, and patience.

1
Fictions and the Construction of the New Relatus

In a project that has to be completed within a short time, how could one create the features it would have if, instead, it were to take longer? This question could sum up this book.

The question arises out of the acceptance of a problem or challenge: the plans arising out of a project—"projects of architectural complexes that go beyond the scale of the simple living unit" as a way of somehow specifying the measure of the scope of this piece of work and avoiding the term "urban planning"—face a difficult challenge because of the way they were projected. When the public space goes beyond the scale of a simple constructed volume and begins to turn into the component of a project, these plans begin to assume another social dimension, and turn into the scenario of social life beyond the program of uses.

There are certain clues pointing to the difficulties faced by the production of collective space when tackling this second task. The difficulty of modern urban planning is to create heterogeneities. Such concerns were most notably raised by Camilo Sitte when Vienna's Ring was being completed.[1] The same theme has emerged as a constant throughout twentieth-century architecture even while different paths were being followed by a diversity of architects that spans the likes of Germany's Theodor Fischer, Hugo Häring, Hans Scharoun and Finland's Eliel Saarinen, Otto-Ivari Meurmann, and Alvar Aalto, just to name a few.[2]

---

1. Collins and Crasemann Collins, *Camillo Sitte.*
2. Blundell Jones, "Discovering Hugo Haring."

This subject, present throughout modernity, has been intensified in a day and age when the pace of construction and development is now beyond any other recent time period in world history. During the building process there are always references to the past, but in the spaces where nothing was built in the past the planner faces an unorganized physical environment. In the recent growth of cities in the places where there is no conception of what was experienced in the past exists, or when the urbanization process itself has wiped out the existing organization (in other words, when swathes of countryside are turned into cities), the only antecedents are physical: topography and geography. The tools and functional needs to transform such spaces, the capacity and need to create large-scale urban transformations within a short period of time, are given a higher value than the capacity of inhabitants to humanize these spaces and make them their own.

The homogeneity of these new architectural developments often hampers the emergence of what is known as genius loci in the field of architecture, and which could be termed ubiety. In other words, the homogeneity of such developments can have a dehumanizing effect. There is no place for the particularities of human scale, and outside the private space of the home it is difficult to make that appropriation of space possible.

A principal aspect linked to heterogeneity can be deduced from the understanding of the city as a memory bank. Events gradually leave behind their traces in the buildings and spaces in between; erosional forces record the passing of time, and the imaginary trace of inhabitants' footprints testifies to the events people have experienced there.

As a consequence of their capacity to preserve recollections and guard against the amnesia of history, architecture is turned into the de facto memory bank of quotidian existence and is filled with meaning. This capacity has been turned into the main tool of classical mnemotechnics.

The fact that architecture can serve as a cultural memory bank has two contradicting aspects: one is that buildings change with the times and become witnesses of the past as remains accumulate there. The other is that, as architecture becomes transformed by new realities and erases the old ones, this tension creates a competition between the old and the new. In this development different scales and interpretations cross each other in multiple, complex realities.

Indeterminacy and Project

A possible response that could be given to the appearance of this shortcoming might be that time will do its work here. After having been lived-in for many years, the new spaces will also accumulate their own experiences: erosion over time will leave its mark on the surfaces of buildings, the use of collective space will change, the direction of traffic on the road will be reorganized, gardens will appear and disappear, the use of some buildings will change while the main structural relationships of the primary spaces will hardly change at all. Faced with this, one common solution is to propose open-ended projects as well as open-ended pieces of art and architecture.

If architectural plans are understood as a general strategy, rather than as closed forms, and if the rules which are their tools for realization leave a margin of flexibility, it is possible to bring into play different points of view that allow a factor of indeterminacy to emerge. In these cases, by giving up some control over a project by allowing a certain amount of indeterminacy, the responsibility for the final result is left to chance. It does not appear that indeterminacy alone could produce a better result, and it is evident that few people are in favor of accepting the risks of doing this. The project planning process continues to be the main tool for controlling the shape of any building.

Formal games and the role of chance are generally restricted to the project planning sphere, to the laboratory work prior to starting to build. If such tools remain restricted within the bounds of the project's development phase, the process itself becomes the best chance to inject creative potentials into the final result.

The project that is understood as a process turns into a record of its development. Its main features will not be so much the formal consequences that it will provide an answer for, but the strategies and methods used in its development. Very often rather than built architecture, it is the project itself that comes under scrutiny, particularly in academic and publishing mediums. The graphic representations of the project have become so important today that a prominent place has been occupied by documenting the development process. The process of a project's transformation largely takes place in the laboratory environment of design.

> The influence that, in recent years, the concept of process has had to establish a theory of the project has been incredibly important. People, like myself, for example, who have spent twenty-five or thirty years in architecture schools can testify how much so many students today insist in process when they present their projects: process, so much so, as responsible for the project. How many times have we hear that what is being done it to register the process, to keep in mind all of the succession of formals states that are offered as a justification for a final and last state? What is interesting, moreso even that the architectural work, is the "biography" of the project, and from there the continuing interest in the testimonial of what was its gestation process.[3]

Paradoxically, the more unique and arbitrary the results of projects are, the greater the level of precision that is demanded in the building resources, so that when the most arbitrary shapes are built, they are realized in the greatest precision. When geometries or techniques that deviate from the usual standards are used, greater specialization is required from the builders. Non-canonical geometries pose special difficulties for measuring and constructing, and thus reduce the margins for error.

Through an algorithm, CAD parametric programs provide an opportunity for the laws of a shape to be established and for the final shape to be obtained as a result of a mathematical function instead of being represented directly. The shape that is achieved through such tools is largely a surprise, since concrete realization is not revealed until the last moment. These new tools have taken the development of geometric shapes out of the realm of prejudice and foreknowledge and into that of exploration and research.[4]

> Today, the idea of erudition, of the architect as connoisseur has been rejected. It is curious that in a world of increasing specialization, where artists and scientists are making dynamic new work from within their disciplines, architects have followed the lead of the management consultant, the ultimate example of the empty generalist. Rather than rise to the tech-

3. Moneo. *Inquietud teórica y estrategia proyectual*, 151. In the chapter dedicated to Peter Eisenmann. Translated by Daniel Montero.

4. The different accessories of the "Rhino" program, for example, enable the conditions that a shape must meet to be specified, and when its algorithm has been composed, to "find" the specific shapes.

> nical and artist; challenges of today, within the discipline of architecture, mainstream practice has embraced the rhetoric of the market to make work that is infused with brand recognition. Strategies of cybernetics, phylogenics, parametrics, mapping -each strive to generate completely original forms, unusual shapes, in plan, in section, sometimes both. These bold profiles can amplify or even replace corporate logos. Lacking the complexities and ambiguities that are held within the tradition of architectural form, these shapes quickly lose their shiny novelty and achieve a condition of not new, but also not old or ordinary enough to become a part of the urban background. This inability to grow old is all too resonant with an era of rebranding and cosmetic surgery. Architecture is now practiced at an unprecedented global scale, and the major players seem te be egging each other on. Who will produce the largest, and most formally outlandish project? Who will finally say stop? Never has so much construction been based on so few ideas.[5]

They constitute a step forward, because they have greatly broadened the availability of possible geometries. When more factors are incorporated into the equation, more complex results become possible. Yet they have their work cut out for them when it comes to taking the leap from the uniqueness of each individual object to a broader scale. At least they have created exceptions in the uniformity of the areas in which the formal catalogues based on canonical geometries once predominated.

New Foundations

Throughout history there are many examples of cities created out of nothing. They were mostly created as a consequence of a new political, religious or cultural setups, on which their structure and organization were based. Despite using regular geometries, mostly abstract reticulations, their ultimate meaning and general organization were conferred on them by that power or aim that caused them to be built. As they were created with the aim of specifically organizing the life of a given society, their basic ingredients were focused on the development of public spaces and institutions. A clear example of this includes, for instance, the cities created out of nothing by the Jesuits

5. Caruso, "Traditions."

in South America, known as the Reductions of Paraguay. With evangelization being the aim, the total organization of life around this aim conferred meaning on that new structure. All aspects of life were organized in accordance with the aim of evangelization to the point of organizing not only the place that each institution needed in the city, but also in the everyday lives of its inhabitants.

> The Jesuits of Paraguay established colonies in which existence was regulated at every turn. The village was laid out according to a rigorous plan around a rectangular place at the foot of which was the church; on one side, there was the school; on the other, the cemetery-, and then, in front of the church, an avenue set out that another crossed at fight angles; each family had its little cabin along these two axes and thus the sign of Christ was exactly reproduced. Christianity marked the space and geography of the American world with its fundamental sign. The daily life of individuals was regulated, not by the whistle, but by the bell. Everyone was awakened at the same time, everyone began work at the same time; meals were at noon and five o'clock-, then came bedtime, and at midnight came what was called the marital wake-up, that is, at the chime of the churchbell, each person carried out her/his duty.[6]

In our day and age, the logic of infrastructures on a territorial level tends to be the basis of the organization and, as far as buildings are concerned, models that can bring about a more viable management of constructability are preferred. Just as in economic plans, the scale of the projects gradually increases beyond the local conditions of topography and environment. The criteria for structuring a new city are in accordance with broader tracts of territory.

The Seeking of Ubiety and the Construction of Fictions

When faced with the difficulty of building new ubieties, known models turn into places of refuge. The evolution in the concept of heritage is an example of that. From being the expression of the survival of glory throughout history, it became the memorial to a lost past, until it became the useful symbol of a forgotten meaning.

6. Foucault, "Of Other Spaces, Heterotopias."

When these memories were lost, or when there was simply no precedent, the building of fictions has been another resource that has been developed. In architecture all the different means have been worked on in the relationship between the object, its meaning and memory. The recollection that was not provided by time was built by means of a fiction, through different means. Imaginary times, distant pasts and places have been reinvented by using materialities that invoke varying degrees of authenticity. The paths of time and place cross each other on certain occasions and yield different kinds of results. These ploys have been accepted by the inhabitants, who have demonstrated that they are ready to participate in these fictional roles.

Other Fictions

The building of fictions is not something that takes place in the sphere of architecture alone, and in the first part of this piece of work I have endeavoured to open up different perspectives on this subject from a number of areas.

The building of hypothetical memories, the composition of imaginary memories with pieces of real recollections, the reconstruction of a forgotten past while pursuing the vestiges of images, are all mechanisms that have been used in many disciplines apart from architecture. The study of some of them can be enlightening and of interest when it comes to different approaches in the field of architecture.

Construction of the *Relatus*

The second part of this work studies three of Frank Gehry's projects. Gehry's way of working in these projects represents a different methodology when set against what has been pointed out above —a way that displays a strategy to create fresh ubieties in a place devoid of precedents. The three projects under consideration are located in Los Angeles. As Rafael Moneo recalls when studying Gehry's work, working in Los Angeles is tantamount to working on a tabula rasa.[7] In such surroundings, to quote Moneo: "His ar-

7. Moneo, *Inquietud teórica y estrategia proyectual*, 257. In the chapter

chitecture (Gehry's) can be understood as a reflection on how to construct the city."

In other words, he points to the way of building a city beyond the single building.

The resources he uses in this task are not fictitious but real; they are the resources of the culture in which the projects are incorporated and those of the author's knowledge. As known resources in universal architecture, they have precedents mainly in the work of Alvar Aalto, among others.

When giving a name to the mode of work used by Gehry in these projects, I propose a concomitance which I have called *relatus*. The results of these projects have the structure of literary narration. The identifiable parts of reality are sewn together by the thread of a cohesive argument. Without creating all the aspects of a complete reality they nevertheless form a coherent whole.

Choice of the Term *Relatus*

When setting out to establish that similarity of structure, I searched for the equivalent of the Spanish term relato. Using the Ereduzko Prosa Gaur (Exemplary Prose Today) data base I discovered that the word *errelato* has been used in several pieces of writing, including Bernardo's Atxaga's novel *Soinujolearen semea* (*The Accordionist's Son*). But as a principle term I did not like it. In the end, I favored the Latin word relatus from which this term is derived. First, because I felt that the appropriateness of the word in this case, is strongly related to its precedents based on the literal meaning. [8] Secondly, because when translated into other languages it would give rise to less confusion, since it avoids the limitations of a more narrow meaning that could be conveyed by narration. When seeking the translation of the word relatus into English, Wiktionary and the Babylon dictionaries gives the following translation: "Nar-

---

devoted to Frank Gehry. "Building in Los Angeles is the equivalent of beginning from zero, of working on a blank slate." ("Construir en Los Angeles equivale a partir de cero, a trabajar sobre una tabula rasa.")

8. On the other hand, irregular verbs often have etymological dual meaning: assim refero, which means "to carry back", reached Spanish as *referir*, and its past participle *relatus* "that which is referred to" originated the noun *relato* and the verb *relater.*" www.elcastellano.org/artic/latin.htm

ration: Telling of events." This "telling of events" aptly defines the meaning I want to give here. Wherever fictions revive the narrations of the past, the new relatus creates the structure of telling an event from scratch, which will constitute the structure of new narrations.

And parenthetically, a note on the term *ubiety* that I have used in this piece of work: the Euskalterm terminology bank gives "ubietate" as a synonym in Basque of the word "lekutasun"—and in translation gives "ubiedad" in Spanish, "ubiety" in English, and "ubiétè" in French.. I found a striking use of it in a passage in Leibniz's *New Essays on Human Understanding*:

> The scholastics have three sorts of *ubiety*, or ways of being somewhere. The first is called *circumscriptive*. It is attributed to bodies in space which are in it point for point, so that measuring them depends upon being able to specify point in the located thing corresponding to points in space. The second is the *definitive*. In this case, one can 'define'—i.e., determine—that the located thing lies within a given space without being able to specify exact points or places which it occupies exclusively. . . . The third kind of ubiety is the *repletive*. God is said to have it, because he fills the entire universe.[9]

In English I found the following definitions, among others: condition in respect of place or location; local relationship; whereness," or "the property of having a definite location at any given time; state of existing and being localized in space."[10]

9. Leibniz, *New Essays on Human Understanding*, 221–22.
10. *Oxford English Dictionary* and *Random House Dictionary*.

2
Precedent and Approaches

Grafting

Five new varieties of apple can be produced from a single apple, a different one for each of the five seeds it has. If all the seeds of an apple tree were to germinate every year, hundreds of varieties of apple would result. Apples of the same species are not obtained from the seeds of an apple tree of a specific variety of apple. This happens because the apple is heterozygous, similar to the way we human beings are, and this feature is extreme in the case of the apple. The apple is believed to have originated in the forests surrounding the Kazakhstan city Almaty. The name Almaty could be translated literally as "full of apples." The Malus sieversii, the eighteen meters high, three-hundred-year-old apple trees can be found there with trunks as thick as those of oaks; they produce fruit of all colors and sizes, from yellow or green to red and purple, ranging from the size of cherries to the diameter of a football. Thanks to its heterozygosity, it has adapted to totally different territories and climates all over the world, because the variety that emerges in each generation enables a variety that can adapt to a new situation to appear.[1]

When chance produces a successful variety of apple, its branches are grafted onto other apple trees so that they will produce the variety of apple one wants to reproduce. That is why all the apples we eat have come from trees that have been grafted, otherwise it would be almost impossible for the new varieties produced randomly to be edible.

1. Pollan, *The Botany of Desire.*

The genetic memory of a fruit that is taken as the model is implanted in the fruit tree by means of grafting. In this case, grafting is a way of overcoming heterogeneity, a way of establishing a known homogenized feature above particular conditions. Similar specimens of known valued species are produced to prevent the diversity and uncertainty that would arise from the reproduction means that is intrinsic to the fruit.

Nexus 6: Grafted versus Naturally Developed Memory

Roy Batty died of humanity. He was the model for humanoids (replicants) created for the toughest of jobs. He was not created to develop human attitudes, yet in the moment he died, this Nexus-6 replicant displayed human emotions.[2] Driven by empathy toward his hunter (Rick Deckard), at the very moment of his death he incongruously saves Deckard from the abyss. In his last words Batty reflects the awareness of his own death, and he perhaps realizes that his recollections will have no other repository than Deckard, and that they will be lost forever. He realizes he will have no successor who will remember his memories. Despite his artificial creation, the lack of continuity to his existence and realization of ending up in grimmest nothingness of death, causes him distress:

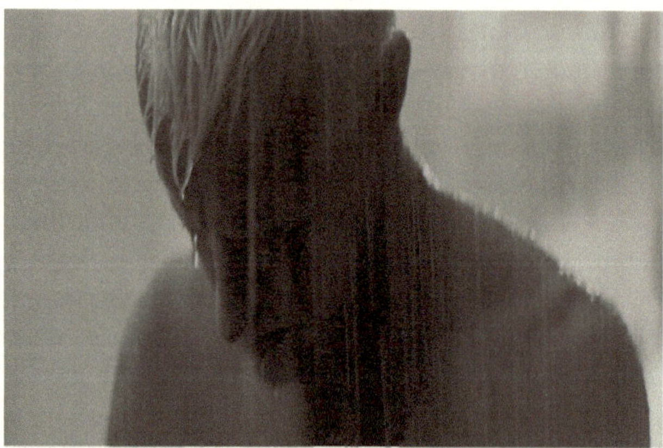

Roy Batty, Blade Runner, *1982.*

2. *Blade Runner*, directed Ridley Scott. Based on the novel *Do Androids Dream of Electric Sheep?* by Philip K. Dick.

> I've seen things you people wouldn't believe. Attack ships on fire off the shoulder of Orion. I watched C-beams glitter in the darkness at Tannhäuser Gate. All those moments will be lost in time like tears in rain. Time to die.

In this conversation of the final moment the brightest experiences are highlighted above all the others, the ones that will be the brightest, most striking, most unforgettable events, and in the recounting of these moments that have been experienced a bid is made to survive, the wish to transmit them to others. On the threshold of his death he is distressed because the memories of his deeds will not be passed on to anyone else.

Memory, among other things, is the door to immortality, a place for the after world. Leaving religious beliefs aside, it is something that enables earthly immortality to be rationally guaranteed. Being able to survive in the memories of others is the most reliable, and maybe only way, of projecting oneself beyond one's own death. This kind of memory somehow involves a whole group of human beings in that chain (in which) we are all strongly linked together.[3] The feeling of empathy binds the individual to that group.

> Deckard (voice-over): "I don't know why he saved my life. Maybe in those last moments he loved life more than he ever had before. Not just his life, anybody's life, my life. All he'd wanted were the same answers the rest of us want. Where did I come from? Where am I going? How long have I got? All I could do was sit there and watch him die."

Being remembered is an intrinsic desire of human beings, just as being forgotten has historically been considered a curse. In Ancient Egypt and Rome there was a punishment called Damnatio Memoriae, literally "damnation of memory."[4] This punishment was handed down on many emperors. When the Roman Senate officially ordered the Damnatio Memoriae, the punishment involved the removal of everything that could recall the person in question–a statue, a monument, an inscription–and the condemned person's name would also be prohibited. The removal of images was de-

3. *Kate horretan denok batera gogorki loturik gaude.* A line from the poem "Izarren hautsa" (Stardust) by the Basque poet and singer Xabier Lete (1944–2010).
4. Padilla Aguilar, "La destrucción del recuerdo."

signed to delete memories. Just as public memorial objects aimed to keep certain events and their protagonists in people's memories, removing them was designed to remove them from people's minds.

The works of human beings are also a route to immortality. This is how the following passage by Jorge Oteiza can be understood, when the author points out in the final notations of the poem "Androcanto y sigo":

> My Dear God: I want to leave you this small stone, this small stone that wasn't among all that You made; now this small stone breaks your solitude, the only thing that breaks it, as the breaking of a great stained glass in which you drew all of the planets and all of the kinds of treats that you created in the universe and which were incapable of saying to you a single word. That all of the constellations continue walking and the minerals apparently more obstinate like men, and the most difficult plants, which they will continue to do like when You let them go from your hand. What does this matter to You? What interest does all of this known and unknown development have for You? But here I have that I discover You, I recognize You, I incorporate You, and I accompany You. Now, yes, You are happy. From this small stone, I also, my God, am happy and I am crying from true happiness. Thinking of you I make this small stone. Where is the river now? That desperate river that pushed me toward death because I could empty myself of You. Now let this river come, and try to wash away this small stone, and it will not be able to.[5]

For humanity, the roots of the past exist in the present in the form of memories. In the epigraph to his autobiography *Living to Tell the Tale*, Gabriel García Marquez says: "Life is not what one lived, but what one remembers and how one remembers it in order to recount it."[6] That "life" is the awareness of oneself which one has built throughout one's personal time, throughout one's physical lifetime.

These roots, following the literal nature of the botanical metaphor, are also linked to their place of origin, and in one way or another are not only compatible, but exist as two sides of the same coin: time-roots on the one hand, and space or place-roots on the

5. Oteiza, *Existe Dios al noroeste*, 47. Translation by Daniel Montero.
6. García Márquez, *Living to Tell the Tale*, frontmatter.

other. The events preserved in memory are remembered at specific locations. We remember the place of the event, for example, as linked in the most indistinguishable way with the occurrence. Because one of the aspects of the event is the space "where it took place," the place and recollection are linked to each other intimately. The key to remembering what happened could be like remembering the place. For the masters of classical mnemotechnics, sight was the most effective means for fixing events in the memory, and techniques that developed the memory at the service of rhetoric were developed on the basis of this capacity.

One way to overcome the problems caused by a lack of roots (or uprooting) could be to build or create roots. But insofar as this "building" or creating can be the substitution or retrieval of something that was in the past and which has been lost, one often speaks of re-creating or re-building. That re-construction implies having existed previously. To retrieve what has been lost, it first has to be lost.

Roy Batty was created by the Tyrell Corporation in the film *Blade Runner*. The Nexus-6 were humanoids known as replicants. They were created to substitute human beings in the toughest of tasks. Their physical and mental capacity was above that of human beings and they were used to operate in extreme conditions of work far away from our planet or, in some cases, for the pleasure of human beings. Although they did not have memories at the moment they were created, Mr. Tyrell realized that as their lives progressed they were capable of developing human behavior out of their own experiences. To prevent that, to stop them from creating their own ways of acting independently, an expiration date was imposed on them, a lifetime of four years at the most.

Aware of that expiration date, a group of renegade Nexus-6 replicants return to Earth seeking a solution that will give them the chance to survive. As their return is illegal, they attempted to mix among human beings and pass unnoticed. This is where the work of the Blade Runners begins: to seek out the replicants, identify them and "retire" them.

The Tyrell Corporation took another step toward solving the problem whereby replicants would be used for other purposes and which could be called Nexus-7. In the creation process, they began to insert hypothetical memories into the replicants. By giving them the memory of another human being and making them believe it was their own, the replicants would regard themselves as human, and on that basis they would be able to build their own nature. In the film, Rachael is the example of this new generation. Eldon Tyrell implanted his niece's memories into her and turned her into his closest colleague. Nevertheless, when Deckard subjects her to the Voight-Kampff test, even though her memories are implants, she fails in the empathy test and is clearly cold and distant in her personal relationships.

Compared with her, the awareness of his own character that Roy has built on the basis of his own experiences appears human, so much so that he feels compassion toward his persecutor. Aware of the limit on his expiration, he returns to Earth and is involved in the quest to find a drug that can give him more life. This fact also indicates that he is aware of the nature of himself, and already feels a desire to survive and rebel against his destiny.

Memory is one of the main features of humanity. One's own memory is constructed from the recollections of experiences and of what is learnt. Edita Mombiela points out in her paper "Sobre la utilidad de nuestra Memoria en nuestra Vida Presente y nuestras Esperanzas de Futuro":

> For various reasons my generation was educated under the slogan "let us replace memory by sense" with the laudable aim of producing individuals that were more autonomous and freer. But it may have ignored the fact that we ourselves, what we call "I," are no more than the result of a process to accumulate memories. Without memory, without reminiscences, we would not be able to speak, nor recognize, not even imagine, insofar as that imagination is no more than the novel reworking of knowledge content that we already possess.[7]

To enable the latest generation of replicants to adapt to society and play the role of humans, they are implanted with an imaginary memory, in some cases a real one, as in the case of the memory of Tyrell's niece that was implanted in Rachael. This enables them to act normally among human beings, but they still do not pass the

7. Mombiela. "Sobre la utilidad de nuestra Memoria en nuestra vida presente y nuestras esperanzas de futuro," XXX. Title translation: On the Usefulness of Our Memory in Our Present Life and in Our Future Hopes. Translated by the translator.

Voight-Kampff test completely. In other words, they do not fully develop an empathy of the type that humans have. Certain behaviors, cultural and habitual, are implanted in them, and insofar as the replicant models are improving, they end up being capable of responding to more questions in the Voight-Kampff test than that of earlier replicants. But they still lack the behaviors that they are supposed to have acquired, ones that are supposed to have been built out of their direct experience. This is reflected in Rachael's relationship with Rick Deckard. On her own she does not create the attitudes she finds in other people, even though she is aware that they should emerge in her. In the final scenes of the film when the two escape to another country, the hope of building this capacity emerges.

> Deckard (voice-over): Gaff had been there, and let her live. Four years, he figured. He was wrong. Tyrell had told me Rachael was special: no termination date. I didn't know how long we had together, who does?

Without having been implanted with these foreign memories, the Nexus-6 humanoids still build human behaviors on the basis of their experiences and the awareness of their artificial nature. The sentiments the replicants display throughout the film are love, hate and mercy, unlike human beings. The moment in which Roy kills Tyrell, or the love that is expressed by Roy himself when Pris dies, the fear and resignation displayed by the latter—are examples of that. In one scene the replicant Pris appears looking at the human J. F. Sebastian, and asks him, "How old are you?" and Sebastian replies, "Twenty-five." But seeing that he looks considerably older, Pris asks: "What's the problem with you?" Sebastian tells him that he has Methuselah Syndrome, a rare glandular disease that accelerates ageing. Later on, Pris and Roy use that knowledge to create a relationship of empathy between them and Sebastian. Pris says, "We have similar problems, accelerated ageing," and subsequently, "You're our best and only friend," and "you're the only one who could help us."

> The replicants are starting to develop a human-like soul, and are shown to express emotions in the film; whilst the humans are losing their souls, and are rarely shown acting emotionally. The exceptions are J. F. Sebastian, an outcast because of a

> genetic defect, and Deckard later in the film—who rediscovers empathy via contact with the replicants. Rachael and Roy are mirrors in which Deckard can assess his humanity. Much discussion of the film has centered on whether Deckard is a replicant or not. In the present reading, Deckard is human, which preserves the doubling symmetry of humans becoming soulless, and replicants gaining souls. The trend towards regarding Deckard as a replicant (a machine rather than human), diminishes the richness of this remarkable film. The final eye imagery is that of Tyrell's eyes being gouged out, by the insightful Roy, suggesting that Tyrell has indeed lost his soul. The replicants, in this case, represent hope for the future, by showing humans how much they have let their humanity slide."[8]

The implanted memories do not guarantee humanity, nor the capacity to feel empathy toward other human beings. They are only a tool for achieving a basic socialization. According to the example of the replicants, full human development would only be based on personal, individual experience. In that respect, the experiences of the individual, direct experiences would be decisive, and among these experiences the most unusual, the most brilliant, the most spectacular, the most remarkable ones would, above all the rest, be the milestones of the new narration that is being built

The Reconstruction of Memory

In Ridley Scott's film, when a past is implanted in a replicant, the props of reality are also created around it: the photos and objects that could have come out of that hypothetical past. Because memory, insofar as it is a process that is continuously being reconstructed, is fed by these.

According to a study conducted at Concordia University, memories change with the passing of time. So memory is not static, but something that evolves every day. All the elements of memory tend to be restructured and organized every day, and the latest structuring is apparently what we remember. Memories do not change suddenly overnight of course, but slowly and gradually. Our favorite

8. Nottingham, *Screening DNA*, chapter 3, section "Androids made flesh: *Blade Runner*."

memories apparently do not escape these changes either.[9]

It is not very clear how these changes take place, but there are some theories. In the words of Jean Roch who led the pieces of research at Concordia University, the brain remembers only the most important events while the details are forgotten. Afterward, when the event is remembered again, the details are invented to complete the event and make it credible. As the brain forgets the origin of the details, any detail read or seen can be added to what is remembered. That way memories change, and even the events that have marked our lives. The most amazing thing is that the person believes he or she truly lived through what is remembered. In other words, he or she believes that the event really happened in the way he or she remembers it.

In Umberto Eco's 2005 novel *The Mysterious Flame of Queen Loana*, when Giambattista Bodoni wakes up in a hospital bed he realizes that he has lost all his memories. He is sixty and does not recognize his wife or his children, he does not know what job he does, what his hobbies are. His friends know him by the name of Yambo, but he has forgotten them.

In this situation his wife takes Yambo to the village of Solara in the Piedmont Mountains to the house where he spent his childhood. The mementos of his childhood and adolescence are kept in the attic there. He is going to reconstruct his past on the basis of those books, comics, discs, magazine articles and film posters. These objects will help him reach the memories that are locked in the past and which now he has forgotten.

We could ask whether the memory he rebuilds is real or not. First, we could ask whether something that is constructed "again" is the same as the original thing. In European culture, from the perspective from which we understand the authenticity of an object, they are not the same thing, inasmuch as the replica and the original thing are not the same. In the case of the Japanese Shinto temples, by contrast, the whole building is systematically built again within a certain number of years, and it does not stop being the "same" temple. In this case, one would have to examine how far the shrine is the building or the place where it is located.

In any case, whether real or not, it would be unlikely to think

9. Ana Galarraga (2001), Joana Mendiburu (2000 and 2001) and Xabier Zupiria Gorostidi's (1996) articles in the magazine, zientzia.net.

that the memory Yambo might build could be considered identical to his previous one. Even for those who have not lost their memories, their memories are continually being rebuilt, they are changeable with the passing of time. What Yambo would build is no more than a new reconstruction; it would be a reassembling adapted to the conditions of his new situation. These memories obtained through objects would continue to adapt according to the recuperation process itself.

In the novel one of the first things the doctor shows Yambo is a photo of his parents, and "Yambo" Bodoni flies into a rage when he realizes that he does not remember them. He knows who they are, because he has been told, but he doesn't remember them: "it is a memory I have been given by you," he tells the doctor and his relatives. In response to this, Dr. Gratarolo tells him: "Who knows how many times you remember because you went on looking at this picture over the last thirty years. Don't believe that memory is like a warehouse that stores memories and lets you take them out just as you fixed them in the past. . . . Memory is a reconstruction, on the basis of what we know or have said in the course of time, too."

Although the situation is totally different, it shares similarities with the character portrayed by Kevin Spacey in the film *The Usual Suspects*.[10] A ship explodes in the port of San Pedro in Los Angeles and twenty-seven bodies appear. The only survivor is the limping Roger "Verbal" Kint (Kevin Spacey). The film opens with him being arrested and interrogated by the police. The plot of the whole film is the story he builds up from his responses to the questions. The film is made up of continual flashbacks between the interrogation and the events of the past, and the main character in the story made up by Roger Kint is the mysterious character Keyser Söze. He is apparently a criminal of Turkish origin. Nobody can follow his tracks—he has been through dramatic experiences, and is only known by a name.

In the end, the detainee has to be released because there is no evidence against him, and he limps out of the police station a free man. But as he walks away from the police station, his limp disappears, and the police inspector (Chazz Palminteri) sits down at his desk, stares at the wall and realizes that throughout the inter-

10. *The Usual Suspects*, written by Christopher McQuarrie and directed by Bryan Singer, 1995.

rogation all the answers given by the detainee, who has just been allowed to go free, have been made up from the newspaper cuttings and information written on the objects posted on the walls of his office. The detainee had built up a complete narrative based on the images and headlines he had been reading in these cuttings.

Just as Eco's Yambo does with the objects kept from his childhood, or in the way that a classical orator builds the discourse using mnemonic techniques from the images located in his memory, Kint built an entire story from the pieces of text hanging on those walls. In this case, it was not the narration of an event that he had forgotten and remembered, but a new structure that he had built. He had created a fiction. That is also the nature of the found-footage technique used in film making.

Found Footage: Imaginary Reconstructions

The short film *Dreamers* was presented at the Berlin film festival by the Iruñea-Pamplona-born film director Felix Viscarret.[11] It is composed of images he took from old documentaries. The narration based on these found images is the life of a hypothetical protagonist and his family, the story of a person who dreamed of flying is built up through the main events that he and his family could have lived through.

What is special about this film is the technique used known as found footage, a narration based on footage that has literally been found. The technique consists of taking different film or documentary excerpts, gathering them together into a new structure and producing a new story. In the case of *Dreamers*, the author uses pieces from old news items, sewn together by the unity conferred on them by old black and white images and speeded up.

All the images put together are "authentic," they are pieces of real news documentaries, which show amazing and historical events. Taking them from here and there, from different origins, and out of their context, a new script is put together within the plot of a new narration. The narration that is built from this new "sewing together" an invention, a fiction made up of pieces of reality. In the context of the new story the old images take on a new meaning, and they build the memory of an imaginary childhood and family

11. See www.felixviscarret.com/dreamers.html (last accessed September 24, 2013).

in the manner of a calendar.

I have a friend who makes films and who lives in Germany; he produces documentaries for television, among other things. Once, when asked about his latest work, he told me: on Saturday and Sunday morning where he lives in the suburbs there are a jumble of sales in which people sell their old possessions. People sell old furniture and other items they no longer need when they move out of their houses. Among the items for sale he finds vintage super-8 film reels from which to build new stories using chosen excerpts.

Alan Berliner of New York could be the most well-known figure in film making who uses this technique.[12] He has won the Emmy award three times. His films *The Family Album* (1986), *Nobody's Business* (1996) or *The Sweetest Sound* (2001) continue to bring him much fame in independent cinema. His latest film is *Wide Awake* (2006) and deals with the subject of insomnia. It was premiered at the Sundance Film Festival and afterward at the Berlin One. In this work he combines all kinds of things: home videos, archive images, television adverts, *making off* material, images of the author himself staying awake, reactions to dreams, and so on. One of his favorite subjects is the family: videos that family members have made of their family celebrations or everyday activities, including the photos they take.

He sews together the images he takes from different sources into a new montage and gives them new words. As is to be expected, in the new film the words do not coincide with the lip movements of the people appearing in the images. When seeing them, it occurred to me that this lack of synchronization must be striking for an English speaker who is used to seeing films and television series in the original version, but not for those of us used to seeing them dubbed. We have already become accustomed to accepting this kind of karaoke in the overlay of fiction. Alan Berliner says he has never written a script himself in all his life, yet he has taken images and tried to find the DNA in them.

Other techniques have also been used to create fictional documentaries. Sometimes the look of a real documentary or the laid-back feeling of negligent staging is created, even though it has been completely planned and performed by professional actors. There are

12. Visit www.alanberliner.com to learn more about this director. Last accessed October 3, 2013.

also techniques that are "invasive" toward the material, images artificially made to look old in order to enhance their credibility, like in the film *Zelig* by Woody Allen, or ones that have been completely altered, like in some of the scenes in Robert Zemeckis's film *Forrest Gump*.

The techniques are different, but the aim is similar, to build a fiction that could give a particular look to the telling of authentic memories.

In the case of the found footage technique, excerpts already filmed are used, images that previously had a different nature, including: excerpts from newspapers, domestic amateur footage, films or other kinds of filmed material. When they are taken out of the original framework and placed in a new context or setting, they take on new meaning. The creator of this technique somehow engages in a kind of DIY (do it yourself). He or she does not follow a plan prepared in detail beforehand, but builds according to the images he or she may come across, relying on what comes to hand, or on what may be found.

In the second case, however, the material is created *specially* for the story. Fresh filming is done, and is given the same makeover so that it looks as if it has been created in another context. That context could have a different format or technique, such as television, black and white, or even a different time period from the past. In these cases, credibility for the different origin of the material is achieved through imitation. The techniques of the format one wants to represent are copied, the damage that would be wrought by time on filmed material are made to happen deliberately. In the case of *Zelig*, the film for these sequences was soiled on purpose and altered so that the main characters appear together with historical figures such as Hitler. In the case of *Forrest Gump* the main character appears with John F. Kennedy and later, with John Lennon.

In these cases there is no intention to deceive. What is created is presented as fiction. Various contextual cues including the passage of time let the viewer know what is happening, or on other occasions, images are incorporated into very well-known historical events of the past.

Nevertheless, there is another kind of virtual reality, which is based on filmed images like those referred to above. It is technically simpler but also much more sophisticated in its subtleness.

In 1994, when the group La Fura Dels Baus performed the work *MTM*,[13] at the start of the show the spectators were confronted with a U-shaped wall made of cardboard boxes that formed a kind of yard inside it. When they arrived, they were given explanations about the performance from a number of screens positioned on top of the wall and some rules and recommendations for its duration. They were invited to relax and dance until the performance commenced.

When the spectators had been dancing for several minutes and gotten into the mood, security service personnel suddenly appeared pursuing someone. They ran after him, caught him and beat him up. It was a very violent event. In the initial confusion the audience did not know whether it was part of the performance or not. A television camera person followed behind the police officers filming the whole scene, which was simultaneoulsy being projected on huge screens. While it was possible to easily follow the violence by viewing it on screen from a safe distance without having to be in the midst of the commotion, the strangest thing was that spectators reported finding the projected image more authentic than what they saw live. It had the familiar format of a television news broadcast. While the images were producing an element of contextual abstraction they were actually experienced as being more powerful than the events being watched live.

Other fugitives appeared after the first one and more people in uniform pursued them. They, in turn, were followed by the cameras. All of a sudden one of the fugitives running away entered a hole in the wall made of cardboard boxes in an attempt to hide, and vanished from the audience's view. The police also went inside the hole after him followed by the cameras. From that moment onward it was only possible to follow the scene by watching them on screen. The events were extreme and very violent and the spectators felt the tension. When the action disappeared from the spectators' view, a tunnel appeared on screen made of cardboard boxes, and the persecution continued within the tunnel. At a specific moment the person fleeing along the tunnel reached an open space, something like a cave. It was full of rats. He was arrested there.

From the audience's perspective there was no gap between the images they saw being filmed live outside, and those they thought

13. Available online at www.lafura.com/web/eng/obras_ficha.php?o=61. Last accessed October 3, 2013.

were being taken in the tunnel. Both were continually being shown on screen. But while the former was authentic, the latter had been filmed beforehand. The protagonists of both episodes were the same, and even though the audience experienced horror, there were in fact no rats in the sports center.

La Fura dels Baus, "MTM." Source: www.lafura.com.

Throughout the work the actors moved the cardboard boxes from one side to another, creating different structures and scenographies at each moment. Toward the end, very gradually and almost without the audience noticing, they built a wall that divided the space into two parts. The spectators wandered bewildered and surprised from one side to the other. As in the persecution sequence at the beginning, the whole performance was offered live on screen with the incorporation of bits filmed in advance. The spectators were able to notice that difference at times, but not at others.

They were divided into two parts by the wall, the images on each side were filmed on camera and displayed on the screens, that way each spectator could not only see what was happening on his/her side, he/she could also follow what was happening on the other side by means of the projections. Depending on what was being shown on the screens, the action on one of the sides gradually died down until it reached a situation in which in the end nothing was going on at all. Whereas on the other side the action started to liven up, the music became louder, and in the end it turned into a Carnival, a riotous party. At that moment the spectators on each side thought that when the wall closed, they had chosen the wrong side; while they ended up in silence, those on the other side were partying. But there was no party, either on one side or on the other. The carnival images had been recorded in advance.

That image often occurs to me while I am watching television. I particularly remember one of those moments during a news program in which hundreds of dish aerials appeared attached to the façades of houses in Albania. They apparently used them for watching the RAI in particular, and according to the news reader, while watching television contests they would dream of the paradise on the other side of the Adriatic.

Here, fiction is built with pieces of reality, as in the found footage technique, but in this case fiction has concealed its true nature. It is not a work of fiction as in the films of Berliner or Viscarret. There are no changes of format or time between the real images and the ones interspersed among the fictional ones. Nothing distinguishes them from each other, because the aim is to create confusion between them.

We were able to see an example of this in the Gulf War. The news programs showed us images of an oil spill caused by the Iraqis, and one of the most moving images was that of a dying bird, trapped in the black oil. Later it was discovered that this particular image had been filmed in Alaska a few years earlier in the Exxon Valdez oil spill. When the viewer is not aware that he/she is watching a fiction, he or she goes on to live in that fiction. Another famous example of this phenomenon happened with Orson Welles's *War of the Worlds* broadcast.

An enlightening description of the possibilities of film montage is found in the writings of Soviet filmmaker Lev Kuleshov during the early 1920s. He describes the technique known as creative geography:

> Khokhlova is walking along Petrov Street in Moscow near the "Mostorg" store. Obolensky is walking along the embankment of the Moscow River—at a distance of about two miles away. They see each other, smile, and begin to walk towards

> one another. Their meeting is filmed at the Boulevard Prechistensk. This boulevard is in an entirely different section of the city. They clasp hands, with Gogol's monument as background and look—at the White House!—for at this point, we cut in a segment from an American film. . . . In the next shot they are once again on the Boulevard Prechistensk. Deciding to go farther, they leave and climb up the enormous staircase of the Cathedral of Christ the Saviour. We film them, edit the film, and the result is that they are seen walking up the steps of the White House. For this we used no trick, no double exposure: the effect was achieved solely by the organization of the material through its cinematic treatment. This particular scene demonstrated the incredible potency of montage, which actually appeared so powerful that it was able to alter the very essence of the material.[14]

Some conspiracy theorists still defend the idea that Neil Armstrong's moon landing was actually shot in a film studio. At the other extreme, gullible tourists take photos of a recently opened theme park believing that it was one of the oldest in the city.

The World Is No More than Five Minutes Old: Projecting An Imaginary Past

In Jorge Luis Borges's "The Creation and P. H. Gosse" the protagonist is the British zoologist Philip Henry Gosse,[15] who published the book *Omphalos* in 1857. The Greek word Omphalos means "navel" and the book recalls an old argument of the early Christians on whether or not Adam, who had been created directly by God, had a navel—given that there would not have been an umbilical cord.

Philip Henry Gosse was keen to find a solution for a problem that had been a source of argument throughout the nineteenth century: the problem of the age of the Earth. He was a member of the Plymouth Brethren and this problem was a source of concern for many who, like him, were Christian believers. The problem boils down to reconciling how God could have created the world in six days given that both geology and archaeology had established that the planet was formed over the course of millions of years.

Gosse provides an answer to the question about Adam's navel:

14. Kuleshov, *Kuleshov on Film*, 52.
15. Borges, "The Creation of P. H. Gosse."

Adam did in fact have a navel even though he had never had an umbilical cord that tied him to any mother. God created him with a navel. According to the principle of reason, each effect has its corresponding cause, and at the same time another effect for this cause, and so on ad infinitum. But according to the resolution chosen by Gosse, in that chain of cause and effect, the events that took place after the moment of Creation would be the only ones that really happened. So the World would have been created by God with the memory of an imaginary past, including memories of events that would never have happened. He called these events, the ones that exist in the memory without having taken place, "prochronic," "outside of time." Borges uses this image in his work to explain their consequences: "there are glyptodont skeletons in the gorge of Luján, but glyptodonts never existed."

In the same line of reasoning, Borges quoted the sentence that appears on the first pages of the Talmudic anthology by the Spanish writer Rafael Cansinos Assens: "It was only the first night, but a number of centuries had already preceded it."[16]

As the Argentine writer states in his text, Bertrand Russell revived Gosse's theory in the ninth chapter of his book *The Analysis of Mind* when he asserts that according to logic we cannot rule out that the world was created five minutes ago.

> In the first place, everything constituting a memory-belief is happening now, not in that past time to which the belief is said to refer. It is not logically necessary to the existence of a memory-belief that the event remembered should have occurred, or even that the past should have existed at all. There is no logical impossibility in the hypothesis that the world sprang into being five minutes ago, exactly as it then was, with a population that "remembered" a wholly unreal past. There is no logically necessary connection between events at different times; therefore nothing that is happening now or will happen in the future can disprove the hypothesis that the world began five minutes ago. Hence, the occurrences which are called "knowledge of the past," are logically independent of the past; they are wholly analyzable into present contents, which might, theoretically, be just what they are even if no past had existed.

16. This and preceding quote, ibid., 24.

Bertrand Russell does not put forward this hypothesis as a real one, but he uses its logical support to analyze the mechanisms of memory:

> I am not suggesting that the non-existence of the past should be entertained as a serious hypothesis. Like all skeptical hypotheses, it is logically tenable, but uninteresting. All that I am doing is to use its logical tenability as a help in the analysis of what occurs when we remember.[17]

In another passage in the same chapter, Russell quotes Henri Bergson when he recalls the two types of memory he distinguishes in his book *Matter and Memory*. Specifically, the example of learning a lesson by heart is used by Bergson to distinguish between the two different phenomena that we understand as memory. When we have to learn a lesson by heart, we read the text many times. As the readings accumulate, we gradually internalize the lesson, until a sort of automatism is created inside us, and through that process we link together a number of events and get into some kind of habit. That habit is not linked to the memory of a specific moment, and we do not link the lesson we have learned with the past.

When we recall one of the readings we did to learn that lesson, a specific reading, our memory takes us to a specific time and place. It calls to mind the image we have stored of that precise moment. The first of the two memories, the one that has been turned into a habit, could be grafted (if that were possible), whereas the second would be "true memory" according to Bergson.

> It is important not to confuse the two forms of memory which Bergson distinguishes in the second chapter of his *Matter and Memory*, namely the sort that consists of habit, and the sort that consists of independent recollection. He gives the instance of learning a lesson by heart: when I know it by heart I am said to "remember" it, but this merely means that I have acquired certain habits; on the other hand, my recollection of, say, the second time I read the lesson while I was learning it is the recollection of a unique event, which occurred only once. The recollection of a unique event cannot, so Bergson contends, be wholly constituted by habit, and is in

17. Russell, *The Analysis of Mind*, Lecture IX. Memory. This and preceding quote both from this chapter, no page number given in online edition

> fact something radically different from the memory which is habit. The recollection alone is true memory. This distinction is vital to the understanding of memory.

As Bertrand Russell points out further on in the same piece of writing, it is necessary to distinguish two things: on the one hand, the memory that is inferred and, on the other, what is based on direct experience. Even though true memory deals with the past, not everything that we know about the past is of that type. Some of the memories are on par with the knowledge we might have about the future. For example, those we can learn from reading a history book, or those which, in Russell's terms, we can obtain from "inferences."

He acknowledges that a precise distinction is difficult, but through an example makes it clear that there are also differences. He uses the example of the people that wander along streets of New York. For instance, I know that right now there are many people in the city's streets, but this knowledge is different if I look through the window and see them directly with my own eyes.

> True memory, which we must now endeavour to understand, consists of knowledge of past events, but not of all such knowledge. Some knowledge of past events, for example what we learn through reading history, is on a par with the knowledge we can acquire concerning the future: it is obtained by "inference", not (so to speak) spontaneously. There is a similar distinction in our knowledge of the present: some of it is obtained through the senses, some in more indirect ways. I know that there are at this moment a number of people in the streets of New York, but I do not know this in the immediate way in which I know of the people whom I see by looking out of my window. It is not easy to state precisely wherein the difference between these two sorts of knowledge consists, but it is easy to feel the difference. For the moment, I shall not stop to analyze it, but shall content myself with saying that, in this respect, memory resembles the knowledge derived from the senses. It is immediate, not inferred, not abstract; it differs from perception mainly by being referred to the past.[18]

Bergson, in his *Matter and Memory*, asserts:

18. Ibid.

> The memory of a given reading is a representation, and only a representation; it is embraced in an intuition of the mind which I may lengthen or shorten at will; I assign to it any duration I please; there is nothing to prevent my grasping the whole of it instantaneously, as in one picture. On the contrary, the memory of the lesson I have learnt, even if I repeat this lesson only mentally, requires a definite time, the time necessary to develop one by one, were it only in imagination, all the articulatory movements that are necessary: it is no longer a representation, it is an action. And, in fact, the lesson once learnt bears upon it no mark which betrays its origin and classes it in the past; it is part of my present, exactly like my habit of walking or of writing; it is lived and acted, rather than represented. I might believe it innate, if I did not choose to recall at the same time, as so many representations, the successive readings by means of which I learnt it. Therefore these representations are independent of it, and, just as they preceded the lesson as I now possess and know it, so that lesson once learned can do without them.[19]

This distinction, once again, takes us to the Nexus-6 of the film *Blade Runner*. According to Bergson and Russell the distinction, in this case, between memory implants (grafted memories) versus those that are acquired naturally, or between "habit" and the "recollection of a unique event," makes clear that only the second would be an authentic memory. What has in fact been experienced, what gathers together known events, is based on the senses, is mostly grafted through images through the principal sense of eyesight. In that respect, it is understandable that classical mnemonics should base its technique on the building of the repository of images.

It is also understandable that, while the basis of memory is made up of the moments "captured" by the senses, the moments revived by those senses in a more lively way should be the ones that turn out to be more firmly grafted. Examples of this are the memories chosen by the replicant Roy Batty in his final conversation. These moments are not ordinary episodes of life, but brilliant events, moments that in some way have constituted milestones in his personal experience.

Grafted memory, on the other hand, would qualify as "habits" in the case of the replicants. According to Bergson, this memory gives

19. Bergson, *Matter and Memory*, 91–92.

us the main tools we need for life, the main competences for physical and intellectual activity, just as we walk and breathe, speak, read and do other things, and perhaps that is why greater importance is attached to it than to what is based on direct experience.

Bergson calls the remembered images image-souvenir. The technique of mnemonics consists of bringing these memories to the foreground and activating them. This process to create mental photographs does in fact belong to the subconscious, and with these techniques the faculty to make it voluntary is developed. For example, being able to remember groups of points at one glance without starting to count them.

Actions, insofar as they push us toward the future, hamper the surfacing of images. On the other hand, in some ways they also prepare the path for them, because they limit the field for all the images we have kept in our memory to the ones that could be related to the perceptions we have at a given moment. These images are continually inhibited by the practical conscience, by the sensory-motor balance of a nervous system existing between perception and action. That memory is waiting for the moment when a crack will appear between the impression of the moment and the movement corresponding to it, to make images pass through it. In these cases recognition is "automatic."

There is another "careful" recognition, which needs the habitual participation of these images-souvenir. A question arises on the relationship between perception and the appearance of memories: do the former cause the latter to emerge mechanically? Or do the remembered images spontaneously come before the perception? The answer can be found in the research done by Goldscheider and Muller on the mechanisms of reading. When challenging those who said that reading is done letter by letter, with the words written on the paper, these researchers showed that reading is in fact a real guessing exercise, an exercise of prediction. Our senses, vision in this case, pick up a number of distinguishing lines and stripes and we complete them with the images we have stored in our memories, creating this illusion by projecting these images onto the paper. So our perception is similar to a closed circuit, the images perceived are continually sent to our "spirit" ("esprit" in Bergson's words) and, in response, the memory-images are sent into space one behind the other.

The habit-memory ends up being inadequate without the other, without direct experience, because past memory corresponds to the second one, and because some images on their own cannot substitute it. What happens in the theme bars has to be remembered, just as old photos perform the function of supposed reminders that could recall past experiences. But insofar as these photographs are false or have been moved, brought from another country and context, they do not make anyone who sees them remember anything. An example of this ocurrs in the film *Blade Runner*, when Rachael, who does not know she is a replicant offers pictures of her past as proof of her childhood, the memories serving as the basis of proposed actual ocurrences when in fact these memories are revealed as "implants." These photos of her youth are anchors that fix and verify her past. But they fail to do so completely because she does not recall the moment when these images were taken, even though she "knows" that the images she sees in the photos are of her past.

As Steve Nottingham points out, when Rachael plays the piano there is a moment in which even though she knows how to play, she finds the movements of her hands strange. Nottingham links this moment with another film, *Mary Shelley's Frankenstein*, in which the newly reconstructed beings notice that their abilities are those of someone else.

> The replicants have a low level of empathy toward animals, for example, unlike humans. Rachael is found to be a Nexus-6, although she thinks she is human. In a later scene, in Deckard's apartment, she fully realizes that she is a replicant, who has been implanted with Tyrell's niece's memories. In this scene Rachael plays a piano and questions whether it is her or Tyrell's niece who is really playing it. A similar scene occurs in *Mary Shelley's Frankenstein* (1994), where the creature plays a recorder and asks where his talent comes from, is it his or derived from the memory of someone he was made from. Deckard tells Rachael that she plays beautifully. She is so much more than just her (false) memory.

The 1970 work by the American artist Joe Brainard *I Remember* is a radical, wonderful expression of the power of memory-images. The whole book is a pure listing of specific sentences, images, smells, places, events, moments and places. The accounts, the narration that will sew these memories together are not built up explicitly. The list of sentences starts with the words "I remember,"and nothing apart from that. Some years later George Perec used the same system to produce his own list "Je me souviens" and dedicated the book to Brainard.

Reading the nearly one hundred and fifty pages containing the memories that Joe Brainard gathered together in his lifetime, the reader gradually builds up an image of the author's life. Sometimes, understanding the full meaning of them calls for knowledge of their cultural context, while others are universal. Through the elements quoted a generation, an era, certain towns and cities, sexual trends, professional activities are built up like a jigsaw, and the reader has to complete them, put them in their context so that they can form a narration.

> I remember the first time I got a letter that said "After Five Days Return To" on the envelope, and I thought that after I had kept the letter for five days I was supposed to return it to the sender.
>
> I remember the kick I used to get going through my parents' drawers looking for rubbers. (Peacock.)
>
> I remember when polio was the worst thing in the world.
>
> I remember pink dress shirts. And bola ties.
>
> I remember when a kid told me that those sour clover-like leaves we used to eat (with little yellow flowers) tasted so sour because dogs peed on them.
>
> I remember that didn't stop me from eating them.
> I remember the first drawing I remember doing. It was of a bride with a very long train.[20]

Just as we are continually reconstructing our memories, we transform the details through time while we retain the main events, so each reading of Brainard is complemented by the contexts of the reader, and each reader builds a biography with different nuances. Each one adds the scenario of his or her similar experiences, and at the end what is portrayed is a mixture of the two, between the ones read and those of the reader. Each reader builds a different biography, the link between Brainard's and his/her own.

---

20. Brainard, *I Remember*, 7.

Following the Tracks: Architecture in the Foundations of Mnemonics

Juanita Carpintero was five years old in 1936 when she was put on a ship together with her sister and two brothers and sent off in the direction of Belgium. She was the youngest of the four siblings.

By that time their father had been imprisoned, and like many other children they were evacuated to another country to safeguard them from the Spanish Civil War. When the vessel called in at a French port, the second of the brothers, aged seven, decided to remain ashore because he did not want to continue the voyage. The other three ended up in Ghent.

While Juanita was in Ghent an elderly couple took her in. That couple had a daughter who was married and living with her husband. Juanita called the daughter and her husband Mama Marta

Basque refugee children from Spanish Civil War, in Gante, Belgium. Source: Juanita Carpintero.

and Papa Gustav, and during the weekends they used to come collect her for picnics at the beach.

Juanita spent four years in Ghent and when she returned home at the age of nine, she and her mother could not understand each other. She had forgotten Spanish, and could only speak Dutch. Her elder brother Vicente became their interpreter. This brother died two years later of tuberculosis, and following the war their father was forced to do hard labour building roads all over Spain. Because of the death of her brother and because she was still a child, Juanita did not keep in touch with her Belgian families.

In 1986 when her son Oskar came home one day she showed him a photograph she had found that day in the newspaper *Egin*. It was an old photo. A group of about a hundred children appeared outside a school. Below it was a four or five-line news item in Basque. She told her son that she had a copy of that photo which she had kept at home, and that she was one of the children in the photo and that she recalled some of the other children. She asked him to translate the news item for her.

Fifty years had passed since those children in the photo had gone to Ghent, and an association set up around them was organising a trip to the Flemish city. Even though she said initially she would not be going, her family persuaded her to change her mind, and at the age of 55 she went on the trip accompanied by her husband. It was a five-day trip and those who had kept in close contact with the families that had taken them in orchestrated the tour. When the day before they were due to return arrived, some of the Belgian organizers asked Juanita whether she could remember any details of the places she had once lived. She described a bridge which she remembered crossing on her way to school. One of the people listening to her suspected which bridge it might be and took them to it. Juanita recognized the bridge the moment she arrived and from there some other houses and spots. They spent several hours in the area trying to remember, but the time to leave arrived and they had to return to the bus station again.

While they were at the bus station a Belgian woman accompanying them saw a local woman, whom she knew, passing by on her bicycle, and called to her. Juanita showed her an old photo she had brought with her and asked if she could recognize anyone. She did, the man in the photo, Papa Gustav, had done his military service with her husband and she knew where he lived, not far from there.

They went to the house and Juanita knocked on the door. The person who opened the door saw and greeted her saying "Juanita!" She was Mama Marta, and she instantly recognized the woman she had not seen since she was nine.

In 2006, a Ghent TV channel came to Donostia-San Sebastian to speak to Juanita and make a documentary about her story.

According to experts, the first traces of memory, in other words, the first connections of neurons, takes place in the hippocampus. The hippocampus retains the neuron connection for a time and after a while they move to the frontal lobe. Apparently the hippocampus is the place where memories are created, whereas the frontal lobe is the place where they reside.

The right stimulus, such as an image, person or event, can be enough to activate the nueral circuit which triggers memory. For Juanita, that bridge held the key to her memories; an image retained to perform the function of an anchor for all the other forgotten memories. It was the point of reference for all the lost scenarios of experience from which she was able to reconstruct a whole sequence of events and, finally, reach the end of her journey.

Mnemonics, the classical art of memory was essential knowledge from classical antiquity up until the eighteenth century.[21] Developed by Simonides of Keos around the year 500 BC, because of what happened when he went to sing at a festival organized by a nobleman named of Scopas of Thessaly.

The story goes that Scopas invited Simonides to his palace to sing a lyrical poem in honour of one of his guests. In a section of that poem Simonides apparently included the praise of Castor and Pollux, and when the moment came for him to be paid, Scopas stingily only paid him half of what he had promised him saying that the rest could be requested from the twin gods to whom he had dedicated half of the poem. Shortly afterward servants brought Simonides a message saying that two young men were waiting for him outside. He went outside and found nobody, but at the very moment he left the banquet, the roof collapsed and apparently trapped and killed all the guests. The collapse was so tremendous that when the relatives of the dead came to look for the bodies of their loved ones in order to bury them, they were unable to recog-

21. See Yates, *The Art of Memory*.

nize them. But Simonides remembered where each guest had been sitting at the table, and thanks to that recollection the bodies could be identified and each family was able to lay their loved ones to rest. The twin gods, Castor and Pollux, generously paid Simonides for the praise he had dedicated to them by getting him out of the place just before the roof collapsed. And this event prompted the basis for the art of memory in the mind of the poet. Realising that remembering where the guests had been sitting had helped him, it occurred to him that a good memory needs an orderly arrangement.

Mnemonics is a technique for remembering that uses the strategy of imprinting places and images onto the memory. It is based on vision, because vision is the most precise of the senses. It was of tremendous importance until the techniques of printing were invented.

In order to store the information that one wants to recall later on, one first has to learn to establish a precise system of places in one's memory. Afterward, images can be stored in these different places. As in the case of Simonides, those places could be real ones, well-known buildings or city centers. The development of this technique led to the evolution of imaginary architecture as the basis for mnemonics.

This art or technique for remembering was to a considerable extent based on architecture. Consequently, as the architecture in vogue at the time was used as the primary mnemonic device, it later corresponded to styles of architecture that were predominent during the classical, gothic or renaissance periods.

Mnemonics was one of the five foundations of rhetoric. To enable the speaker to store the contents of his speech in his head, he had to build a sequence of places in his memory that contained an object that represented the concept or idea that was to be recalled. So when the moment came to deliver the speech, he had to mentally go through those places and retrieve the images one by one to be able to reconstruct his speech. A sword would prompt the mention of a battle or war, gold coins wealth or a prize, etc.

For this purpose the particular locations had to be special and clearly defined, with various distinguishing features that could serve as a route for the retrieval of ideas that could be visited in an orderly way at the moment they were retrieved. According to Quintilian, the building had to be as broad and varied as possible, full of ornaments offering numerous loci, a locus being a place where memories can be easily captured.

The collection of constructed loci could be used over and over again to store different topics. The main feature of these loci was that they should not be too similar, ensuring ideas would not get mixed up. The prescribed distances between various loci was supposed to be regular without being too close.

The images that are stored along this imaginary route are the symbolic marks or shapes of what one wishes to recall. The images used, the imagines agentes, need to be as lively as possible; striking, out of the ordinary, vivid owing to their beauty or ugliness. As Cicero pointed out, "because we remember something that is uncommonly wicked, offensive, amazing, huge, unbelievable or amusing for a long time, when we hear or see them."

The most outstanding example of mnemonics that I have come across in our day and age is the one in the book *Hogeita bina* by the extempore Basque verse maker Andoni Egaña when he explains how he uses the "daisies" technique to organize rhyming groups for verse making. As he is not satisfied by long lists of words, he organizes each rhyming family into a kind of daisy. The "ANA-AMA" rhyme on, for example, is a flower that has seven petals and a center, and on each one an average of five words are stored. He puts the most useful words in the middle, ones that can be inserted at any moment, ones not too specific, and around them he opens up different petals based on many kinds of criteria. In the first one, the ones that rhyme with "arma-arna"; the second comprises those of "Bilintx";[22] he fills the third with adjectives; the fourth with abstract words or words with double meanings; the fifth ones that come from verb forms; in the sixth the ones derived from Spanish; and finally in the seventh, fairly ordinary words that are never used in verses.[23]

Andoni Egaña apparently has between sixty and seventy flowers in his head. He explains how verses are composed using this method thus:

> When I am composing a verse, from a methodological perspective it is a great advantage for me to be in possession of this

22. Nickname of Indalecio Bizkarrondo, Basque extempore verse maker of Donostia-San Sebastian, 1831–1876.
23. Egaña, *Hogeita bina*.

form of organisation. If I just had words in a list, I would have a greater chance of repeating them, in other words, to repeat a rhyming word in the same verse. I always keep the middle bit for towards the end. I know that those words in the middle are the most versatile ones. They will get me out of tight spots as the verse progresses and as I run out of breath and ideas. The benefit of organizing, however, goes beyond that. When I go from petal to petal I know that I will have greater possibilities of saying different things. Sometimes the word itself will suggest to me what to say, and other times I just start speaking and as I search the petals for the exact word I need, the beginning of the sentence will present itself to me.

These ambiguities, redundancies and deficiencies remind us of those which doctor Franz Kuhn attributes to a certain Chinese encyclopaedia entitled 'Celestial Empire of benevolent Knowledge'. In its remote pages it is written that the animals are divided into: (a) belonging to the emperor, (b) embalmed, (c) tame, (d) sucking pigs, (e) sirens, (f) fabulous, (g) stray dogs, (h) included in the present classification, (i) frenzied, (j) innumerable, (k) drawn with a very fine camelhair brush, (l) et cetera, (m) having just broken the water pitcher, (n) that from a long way off look like flies.[24]

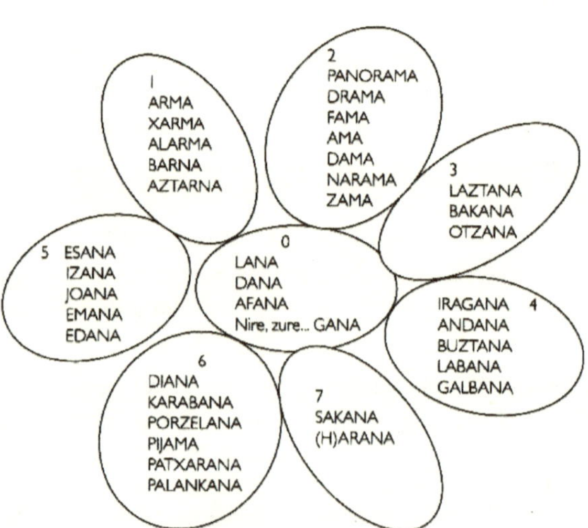

One of Andoni Egaña's "flowers." Source: Andoni Egaña, Hogeita Bina.

24. Borges, "The Analytical Language of John Wilkins," n.p., Internet ed.

Benefits and Disadvantages of History

This story came to me through an acquaintance whose work involves renovating artistic heritage. It took place during the work to renovate a church in Gipuzkoa.

While the church was being restored, the baptismal font was moved elsewhere, to some warehouse, so that it would not get damaged. It was said to be the church's original font, and like the church itself, bore the marks of many centuries.

When the repairs and renovation work was about to be completed, that font was brought back to its original place, so that it could be set up once again on the spot that corresponded to it. When they unloaded it from the lorry and removed the wooden frame, plastic and cardboard, the contractor very proudly showed everyone the restored font. Without telling anyone, he had taken the font to a lathe and had it machined to remove the rough edges and cracks and leave it "as good as new."

I remember my stomach turning the first time I heard that story. When this incident was broached in the course of a conversation with friends about protecting the heritage, the repairs carried out by the contractor with the best intentions in the world struck us as being the most savage intervention imaginable.

Shortly after hearing the story, I had the opportunity to tell it to another friend, and while I was repeating it to him, my stomach started to turn again. But following the initial shock, another thought occurred to me: how upsetting and painful it is to be sensitive about these matters, and how happy are the people who, like that contractor, do not feel this burden.

When I told my friend what had happened to the font, he had recently published the Spanish version of the book *The Botany of Desire: A Plant's-Eye View of the World* by the American writer Michael Pollan. This splendid book is divided into four chapters, each one about a different plant: apple, tulip, marijuana, and potato (which we were told when we were children was the apple of the earth), and in it I came across an unexpected little treasure.

In a section of the chapter written about marijuana, it tells of the research carried out on the way in which the THC component of cannabis affects the brain. How this substance imitates the function of the cannabinoids of our brain, and how its function is mainly to help one forget. According to these conclusions, the cause of "forgetfulness" could underpin the state of perception created by marijuana, and as a result of this, open the doors to a sharper awareness of the present. Linked to the capacity to forget, Michael Pollan cites a work by Friedrich Nietzsche, from the essay entitled "The Use and Abuse of History," written in 1876.

Friedrich Nietzsche tells us at the beginning of his work:

> Consider the herds that are feeding yonder: they know not the meaning of yesterday or to-day; they graze and ruminate, move or rest, from morning to night, from day to day, taken up with their little loves and hates, at the mercy of the moment, feeling neither melancholy nor satiety. Man cannot see them without regret, for even in the pride of his humanity he looks enviously on the beast's happiness. He wishes simply to live without satiety or pain, like the beast; yet it is all in vain, for he will not change places with it. He may ask the beast—'Why do you look at me and not speak to me of your happiness?' The beast wants to answer—'Because I always forget what I wished to say': but he forgets this answer too, and is silent; and the man is left to wonder.[25]

Nietzsche said, "One who cannot leave himself behind on the threshold of the moment and forget the past, who cannot stand on a single point, like a goddess of victory, without fear or giddiness, will never know what happiness is; and, worse still, will never do anything to make others happy."[26]

In his opinion, a person can almost survive without memories, and be happy too, but on the whole it would be impossible for him or her to live without forgetting. Nietzsche goes on to state: "there is a degree of sleeplessness, of rumination, of 'historical sense,' that injures and finally destroys the living thing, be it a man or a people or a system of culture."[27] There is a limit beyond which the human being, country or culture has to forget the past so that it does not turn into the gravedigger of the present. And he proposes the concept of "plastic power" in order to specify this limit or level. This power would be the capacity to grow on one's own, to assimilate the past and what is strange, to heal the wounds, to replace the losses and rebuild the forms that have been destroyed. There are some

25. Nietzsche, "The Use and Abuse of History," section I, 7.
26. Ibid., 8.
27. Ibid., 10.

people who sink as a result of a single painful experience, as a consequence of a slight injustice. There are those who bleed to death from a slight wound, while others are unmoved by the most serious misfortune and brutality of life.

The stronger the roots of the inner being of a human being, the more he or she would assimilate and assume the past. The one who is capable of acting without the limit of history, forgets what he or she cannot control. After it has been forgotten it no longer exists for him or her and remains complete and closed, complete in itself. Both in the case of the individual and the country, a healthy and fruitful life can only exist on this side of a specific horizon. A limit is needed to distinguish between what is accessible and clear on the one hand, and what is unknowable and dark, on the other. But the individual also has to know, in an appropriate way, what needs to be remembered and what needs to be forgotten.

The capacity for feeling in an ahistorical (non-historical) way is the atmosphere life needs to develop and bear fruit. And at the same time, the human being is only human when, through thinking, he or she is capable of imposing limits on that ahistoricity—of using the past as a resource for life—by transforming the past into fresh History.

In Nietzsche's view, people stop being human beings with historical excess. At the same time, mere ahistoricity could be the most unjust situation in the world: narrow, ungrateful toward the past, blind in the face of risks, turning a deaf ear to warnings. Out of this second situation would emerge all action or act, both unjust ones and above all just ones. The artist for his work, the military for their victory. For any country to achieve its freedom it should first desire to escape from such an ahistorical situation. As Goethe famously said, "The doer is always conscienceless, only the spectator has a conscience."

By contrast, the one who is capable of grasping this situation, would be in a different situation, in a "suprahistorical" situation, in a more elevated watch tower. That clear, precise view of history could clearly teach us something: that the greatest and most excellent spirits of the human race do not realize in what chance and arbitrary way they have managed to structure what they see and what they desire to make others see.

Courage would be more necessary than wisdom. History, if it

were to become mere, sovereign science, would lead to the end of life for humanity. If it is accompanied by a vigorous current in favor of life, then it would be healthy and fruitful. There is a situation of historical oversaturation that destroys and degenerates life, and history itself, too. But life needs the service of history, and Nietzsche distinguishes in his essay three ways of dealing with this history: monumental, antiquarian, and critical.

From the monumental perspective, history is exemplary. It is where the powerful can find models in the hope that grandeur existed at one time, it can happen again. When monumental comprehension becomes predominant, only isolated adorned moments are remembered from the past, and many remembrances from ancient events are forgotten. Monumental history tricks us through analogy and can push powerful people to be irresponsible and move the courageous to fanaticism.

The clearest example can be found in the field of art in the difficulties that are placed in the way of those who are capable of truly learning from life and returning what they have learned with a more elevated activity. The creator would always be at a disadvantage in relation to those who are simple observers, in the same way that the armchair politician has been portrayed as wiser than the ruler of the state. The ultimate aim of art experts, those who give precedence to the monumental perspective of the past, would be not to create monumentality again. Instead of saying, "Look, grandeur is already there," their slogan would be this: "Let the dead bury the living." Once again, to echo Goethe: "There is something cadaverous about history, even the best, it smells of tombs."

When criticizing the actions of the scientists in his day, he compares them with the hens forced to lay more eggs, believing they have lost their harmonious nature, "the eggs are always smaller, though their books are bigger."[28]

The second perspective of history, the antiquarian, is that of the person who keeps and adores his or her history, the one that clings to the fatherland and traditions. He or she turns the history of his city into his or her own. He or she identifies with the soul of his or her country above the transience of life. His or her virtues include competence for empathy and the ability to perceive the tracks of a forgotten time. History understood in this way turns into the

28. Ibid., 64.

refuge of countries in times when they have to endure the worst conditions, in the most difficult moments. It protects against the damage of exile, foreignness and uprooting.

Nevertheless, it is not the best situation for conducting scientific research on the past. The sense of the antiquarian is short-sighted, and could attach too much importance to peculiarity. Its main risk: to adore what is old and past, while pouring scorn on what is new and changeable.

When the sense of the people is thus turned to stone, when history is turned into the servant of the past to the detriment of the future, life is mummified. One of its symptoms would be the blind passion to make collections that takes place on some occasions. The history of antiquity undertakes to keep and maintain life, not to create it, and it can paralyze the man of action.

That is why a third perspective is needed, the critical one, this too should be at the service of life. To live, the human being needs strength to destroy the past and liberate him or herself from it. He or she has to be capable of using it on occasions. At those moments it will not be the drive of justice that judges the past, but life itself. According to Nietzsche, "It requires great strength to be able to live and forget how far life and injustice are one.."[29] Luther is credited with saying on one occasion that the world could have been created as a consequence of an oversight of God, because if He had borne in mind the horrible things that exist, He would not have created it.

This last process is also risky, because we cannot free ourselves completely from the chains of our past. Despite judging the aberrations of the past, we cannot deny we are the heirs to it.

> At best, it comes to a conflict between our innate, inherited nature and our knowledge, between a stern, new discipline and an ancient tradition; and we plant a new way of life, a new instinct, a second nature, that withers the first. It is an attempt to gain a past a posteriori from which we might spring, as against that from which we do spring; always a dangerous attempt, as it is difficult to find a limit to the denial of the past, and the second natures are generally weaker than the first. We stop too often at knowing the good without doing it, because we also know the better but cannot do it. Here and there the victory is won, which gives a strange consolation to

29. Ibid., 29.

> the fighters, to those who use critical history for the sake of life. The consolation is the knowledge that this "first nature" was once a second, and that every conquering "second nature" becomes a first.[30]

In the last chapter of the essay he proposes classical Greece as an exemplary example. In his view, the Greeks would be amazed to see the definitions of "cultured" and "historical cultured" being equated with each other in modern times, because for them it was possible to be "cultured" without having any historical education. As Nietzsche said, insofar as the Greeks were the heirs to the heritage of the East, their culture down the centuries was the chaotic merging of different forms from outside, whether Semitic, Babylonian, Lydian or Egyptian, and their religion was the struggle among the gods of the whole of the East. However, Hellenic culture would not have been the mere aggregate of all these, thanks in its view of the Apollonian maxim. The Greeks learnt to bring order to that chaos, reflecting on their needs and themselves, and in accordance with the Delphic doctrine, they allowed their apparent needs to be exhausted, they became their own masters and they enriched and increased the heritage they inherited. The lesson deduced from all that is the achieving of the Delphic maxim: "know thyself." Each one has to reflect on his or her own needs and bring order to his or her inner chaos.

In the case of landscape, the example of the creation of this "second nature" is clear, the proof of this lies in the difficulties and confusion when it comes to establishing the meaning of the very word "natural." In the novel "England, this England" by Julian Barnes, the rich tycoon, Jack Pitman, sets up on the Isle of Wight a new England that will bring together the most intrinsic features of the original England. It will be a replica, which gathers together the most distinguishing elements, which will preserve the essence of all things which not only the local people but also foreigners regard as characteristics of the country. While they are discussing the details of the project, one of his assistants casts doubt on the authenticity of the new reality: to what extent will that copy of the original be credible? Sir Jack Pitman loves to walk in the rural areas of England and gives him the example of what he saw on one of his walks, as a way of showing that what they are going to offer is not going to be

30. Ibid., 30.

a theme park, nor a copy of the other, but the same thing:

> 'And Nature made the countryside as Man made the cities?'
> 'More or less, yes'
> 'More or less, no, Mark. I stood on a hill the other day and looked down an undulating field past a copse towards a river and as I did so a pheasant stirred beneath my feet. You as a person *passing through*, would no doubt have assumed that Dame Nature was going about her eternal business, I knew better, Mark. The hill was an Iron Age burial mound, the undulating field a vestige of Saxon agriculture, the copse was a copse only because a thousand other trees had been cut down, the river was a canal and the pheasant had been hand-reared by a gamekeeper. We change it all, Mark, the trees, the crops, the animals. And now follow me further. That lake you discern on the horizon is a reservoir, but when it has been established a few years, when fish swim in it and migrating birds make it a port of call, when the tree line has adjusted itself and little boats ply their picturesque way up and down it, when these things happen it becomes, triumphantly, a lake, don't you see. It becomes *the thing itself*.'[31]

As Nietzsche said, the hope of those who have the courage to change reality is that this second nature will one day win, and one day will become the first nature.

Credibility is one of the keys to becoming first nature. As Philip K. Dick said in the preface to his first collection of short stories, science fiction and fantasy are distinguished from each other by credibility. He said science fiction deals with "that which general opinion regards as possible under the right circumstances."[32] And we would be talking about fantasy when the reality which is described is considered impossible by the reader, while we would be talking about science fiction when he or she regards it as legitimate or at least possible. What science fiction reflects would not be the reality we experience, but another credible variable of that reality, which could be possible.

When we speak of a landscape, we should remember that the human perception is not invariable either, but quite the opposite. Insofar as the human being, the subject changes. The perspective he

31. Barnes, *England, England*, 62–63.
32. Dick, *The Collected Stories of Philip K. Dick*, vol. 1, *Beyond Lies the Wub*, xiv.

or she has about that nature, changes. Like many former farmers, my late grandfather found it difficult to believe that it was possible to walk in the mountains for pleasure. He found it difficult to accept that what had been his place of work could be regarded as a source of pleasure by his descendents.

Another way for the second nature to be victorious is the adaptation of the human being, the capacity to adapt to the new reality and to develop his/her experiences there. As defended by Oscar Wilde in his essay "The Decay of Lying," nature imitates art.[33] Such dawns and dusks are there owing to the works of impressionist painters, the mists that we can sometimes find are due to the painters. The eye of the human being develops together with his/her knowledge, and that first nature could become a second one without any objective change. The change in vision could function in two senses, to create a new perception of one and the same reality, or as a tool to adapt to a new reality.

In his text Nietzsche referred to the need for forgetfulness, and so did Philip K. Dick in his last lecture given in Metz, when he recalled a passage from the Old Testament which he found fascinating: "For behold I create new heavens and a new earth: and the former shall not be remembered, nor come into mind (Isaiah 65:17)." According to the interpretation of that passage, memory can be a curse when the memory of things that have disappeared are kept, and paradise could have something of the unconscious happiness of the ruminating animals that Nietzsche observed. Or of the frame of mind of that stonemason who had proudly machined the baptismal font.

In the field of architecture, in his Entretiens Viollet-le-Duc himself warned against the obstacles that the memories of history can establish. He proposed deliberate forgetfulness as the only way of overcoming them. He, too, thought that the burden of history could become too much here, and even render the creation of new works impossible:

> I don't know who said that memory was the only paradise we could not be thrown out of. Yet memory is not always paradise, because it reminds us of unpleasant matters, events that have been painful to us, the recollection that renews the guilt for things done badly. Nevertheless, and on the whole, it

---

33. Wilde, "The Decay of Lying," 40–45.

tries to put the bad on one side and keep the good. It's a good friend. I would say that it always acts for our benefit, even when it reminds us of some guilt: very likely it is drawing attention to some debt we ought to pay.

As we now know, they say it will soon be possible to manipulate memory: by taking a molecule called ZIP, it seems we will be in a position to delete unpleasant memories.

At first sight, it makes one afraid. Yet the news is not that frightening: we have acquired tremendous skill when manipulating collective memory, so why not govern personal memory in accordance with our own desires?[34]

Jeanologia: The Erosions of Imaginary Time

"Jeanologia" could be the name of a subject in sociology that might study the iconography developed in the twentieth century surrounding jeans. It would study how these garments, created in America as durable workware, spread all over the world because their ordinariness was valued.

But Jeanologia is the name of a company. It was set up by Enrique Silla in Valencia, Spain. This company developed a technology to age new jeans "instantly," and 400 million pairs of jeans out of the 5 billion currently sold every year worldwide have their look transformed using the technology developed by this company.[35]

The fashion of buying jeans with a used look arose during the last quarter of the last century. It has always been accepted that these trousers are more comfortable and softer after having been used for a time, and what makes them more attractive is largely their capacity to adapt to the wearer's body and movements as they age.

The first step in the new fashion was to sell the trousers in a softened state. This overcame the initial discomfort caused by their stiffness when they are first worn and the shrinking caused by their first washing. But in addition to comfort, another value was high-

34. Anjel Lertxundi in one of his "Hitz beste" daily columns published in the newspaper *Berria* in April 2009 (translated from Basque into English by the translator).
35. See www.jeanologia.com/en/about/ (last accessed October 3, 2013).

lighted: the beauty of the marks and "stains" caused by use. An aspect of that beauty is the "memories" accumulated by those trousers, the object. The movements and experiences of the wearer somehow end up "written" into the tears and creases of the blue denim fabric over a considerable period of time.

That hard fabric which we struggle to squeeze into the first time we wear them, later turn into a garment that fits us uniquely and which we love more and more as time passes,—so much so that we are relcutant to start the whole process over again with a new pair of jeans. In fact, sometimes people prefer to buy a second-hand pair of jeans precisely to avoid the process of breaking in a new pair.

The "used" jeans look has its own socially accepted objective beauty which has led to the creation of "stone" washed jeans. With the new treatment the cotton, instead of fading in a uniform way, loses the most color on what would be the most worn spots when used, thus approximating the look of having been used. After that, other techniques are used to add to the worn affect. Ironing by hand, eroding with sand, spraying with different chemical products all give the jeans their sought after look.

The Velencian Enrique Silla, the CEO of the company Jeanologia, took another step. His aim was to create the used look of the jeans in an authentic way, and he came up with a method that used laser rays.

One day at the end of the 1980s while he was driving from Madrid to Valencia, he stopped at a little village in the province of Cuenca called Iniesta. There he saw two workers picking grapes wearing old Lois jeans of the 1970s, which looked "genuine" to him. The garments were totally ruined by the work, they had the traces of a wallet in the back pocket and Enrique Silla decided he wanted them. He went up to the wearers and offered them new jeans in exchange for the old ones. After thinking he was out of his mind, they gladly accepted his offer. Today they are the prize articles in the collection made up of over three hundred pairs of used jeans. He got hold of some more in India during a trip there, and in a similar deal he exchanged some Lee jeans with a hippie.

What he does with those old jeans is quite simple: he takes a picture of them and after processing it using Photoshop he gives a machine instructions so that the appearance of the jeans can be cloned onto a pair of new jeans, and that way they assume the appearance of "vintage" ones.

To produce the template, thousands of pairs of jeans have been collected at his company over the years. The new technology has enabled the company to "mark" a new pair in the space of thirty seconds.

The oldest item kept in his collection was a pair found in a mine. After cloning them they have been kept in a vacuum pack.

On the label of a jacket this is what I read:

> This garment is produced dyed in piece, with the most advanced "garment dyed" processes and technologies. The "weathered" look and eventual non-uniformity in the fabric is its main feature. Wash with water at 30° without solvents, separately, reverse side.
>
> The style and design of the garment have been manufactured by using industrial processes with pieces dyeing which gives a particular "lived in" look.

In the French version that "lived in" has been translated as "vécu," or "lived."

This text makes it fairly clear what the meaning and beauty of that aspect consists of objects—trousers, furniture, footwear or any garments—do not just appear as used, but as "lived in," and therefore have the memory of a life incorporated into them.

The Ghost's Shoes

The appeal of the used appearance has passed from trousers to other garments. Something similar has happened to footwear. A few years ago the manufacturer Prada marketed some unusual footwear for men. Like all the products manufactured by the firm they were luxury items made of top quality leather and elegant, classical, narrow shoestrings. They were shiny but the strange thing about these models was that the toes had been scuffed. Scuffed new shoes were sold as if someone else had already worn them, marked in such a way that they might have been scratched by a child playing football or dragging them along a surface. Today, in the 2010/11 winter season, we can find shoes in any shoe shop with a "used" appearance.

Getting into clothes used by someone else signifies taking his or her place. The wear and tear caused by that person's use is appropriated, and the memory that is added to the object is displayed as if it were one's own.

Jorge Oteiza used to say that an empty space that had once been full and which had then been emptied was never the same as an empty space that had never been full. The space that has endured occupation followed by de-occupation, the emptying, would remain activated and keep the memory of the previous presence. That perception is evident with the spaces that display traces of having been lived in, places that have accumulated a long history and have been the scenario of many events develop their own character. Beliefs about ghosts haunting palaces and castles would constitute an extreme awareness of these traces.

Footwear and trousers, too, are minute spaces. We can understand them as wearable "places" to live in. The fact that they have been used by someone else before fills them with memories. For reasons of functionality or hygiene it is advisable that someone should be an imaginary person, except in the cases of extreme fetishism or idolatry.

In a paper published in 1992, the architects Antonio Arean, José Ángel Vaquero, and Juan Casariego made an interpretation of the phenomenon of aged jeans that had just emerged at that time. They said "stone-washed" jeans had been an invention of the "western marketing intelligentsia."[36] In their view, the concept of speed dominated the culture of advanced industrial societies by the end of the twentieth century. In that atmosphere citizens would therefore not have time to live their own lives, and would have to borrow another one from elsewhere. But, paradoxically, that borrowed life, has no life. It is sterile. A process that takes a few minutes substitutes another that should take months of life. The genetically modified seeds produced by the multinational Monsanto and which produce sterile plants could serve as a metaphor in this case.

This quest for the aged look is a mechanism that has been accepted. It is true that old things have always had a market. Many people like to fill their houses with antique furniture to give a new house the appearance of another age, or simply to create the "lived in" atmosphere, like that of a well worn jacket. Perhaps because through the presence of an object from the past they put themselves above the passing of time, because the date when they moved into that abode has been deleted. These objects have been incor-

36. Arean, Vaquero, and Casariego. "Madrid 1 tiempo 2."

porated into a memory of the technique or fashion that was in vogue at the time they were manufactured, in addition to the traces of events they have gone through: evidence left by bleaching and dampness in that ageing process, damage caused to them by an absent-minded owner, repair done by a skilful carpenter, etc. In the antiques market authenticity is the guarantee of value, a specialist confirms the origin and period, and the market value is recognized in accordance with that.

Yet the "manufacturing" of antiques is being applied to many other products, too, just in the way it was applied to jeans. Objects that conceal the deception of supposed antiqueness must have always existed. Yet now the process takes place openly, and, what is more, is accepted.

Theme pubs and restaurants have sprung up in all towns and cities. They are of different styles, for example, Irish, English, Bostonian. The most successful in this group are of Anglo Saxon origin. They contain furniture that has the appearance of a specific age, of the early years of the industrial era, but in all cases they predate the new types of material and manufacturing methods ushered in by the Second World War. To that décor complementary elements are added: scruffy black and while photos of old sportsmen, and metal signs written in English, to name two examples.

There is nothing new about using styles and techniques from the past. These revivals, or revisitings, have taken place to a considerable extent in architecture. But in this new trend that we are examining, these elements have to give an appearance of "authenticity," and that is why they have to be damaged so that they look as if they have been used for years. Here the word "authentic" is not the synonym of "true," but of "credible." The aim is to make one believe that these objects, the furniture, the photographs, the paintwork, the advertisements, are antique. In some way, to cause a fiction to be experienced as reality.

On industrial premises that are somehow much closer to them than their hypothetical origin, many workers have spent hours scratching, kicking, filing, hitting and damaging these items, so as to speed up the process of erosion that they would be subjected to by time.

In a pub I know, what stands out on the banisters and on the woodwork adorning the walls are the hammer blows systematically made by the carpenter after the work had been completed. Unlike something that happened randomly, the marks are uniformly spread all over the surface, and if one looks carefully it is clear that the wood is new and that the blows have been administered on purpose. But if one is there without paying much attention, the whole atmasphere comes across as credible.

The key lies in credibility. Scenery is composed for life with similar techniques to those that could be employed by the artistic director of a film to add atmosphere to a scene. The customers know the pub is new, because until a few years ago on the same spot there used to be a café with "modern" 60s décor where retired women would spend hours sitting on the chrome furniture there.

World Press Cafe, exterior and interior (inset)

But that café fell into decline, it became obsolete, and since it was taken over by the new "antiqueness" it has been the most successful in the city. I have seen a tourist taking a photograph of it, happy at the thought of finding one of the city's few memory banks.

Despite not believing it, it is nevertheless credible, just like the jeans aged by Jeanología. To paraphrase the words of Bertrand Russell "the world sprang into being five minutes ago." That is why Enrique Silla goes all over the world gathering samples bearing the clearest traces of having been used, because on an assembly line it would be difficult to repeat the change in colour and crease left in the back pocket by a certain wallet randomly. That effect can only be achieved to a sufficient degree through cloning the real items that bear those stains using a laser.

The pub's customers do not know who that tennis player with the drooping moustache in the old photos is, or that cricket player, for that matter; most have a vague idea what cricket is, but for the moment they are in the midst of a new reality, full of memories, and which has the smell of age just as if the customers had got on a plane and arrived in London or Dublin. They think they are copies of the ones there. Yet most of the ones there, similar to the ones here, are in fact franchise products of recent creation.

But those pubs, jeans and furniture are successful. People use them and we could examine the reason for that success. We are prepared to accept fraud.

Arean, Vaquero, and Casariego took the same principle used on the jeans to the sphere of architecture. They say that the vestiges left by time on the materials used to build architecture not only report on past time, they also disclose whether or not the buildings have their own life. When we walk on old marble pavement, we can see the goodness of the stone, but we can also interpret the wounds written on its surface, the footprints and marks left on the surface by other travellers down the ages. But the same thing does not happen with other materials that have substituted it to perform the same task. They lack that "nameless quality" and time leaves no marks on them. They simply wear away, are damaged, and are replaced in response to a consumer need. Architecture also has this nameless quality, and time is the only variable that enables one to know whether it has value or not. What is often being built is architecture for immediate consumption with an image anchored in a very limited time space and cultural materials that are extremely poor, and which time will soon expose. They say it is architecture that lacks dignity, which has come about to replace something previously that often had pride. Anecdotes produced out of a passing fashion are soon made to disappear by time, and their true nature is exposed. In one case there is life, and architecture makes its voice heard, while in the other, in their words, it is a vertical corpse from the very moment it was created.

The poor material quality and limited shelf life of fresh proposals or contemporary ones could account for the return to the old models and the success of theme proposals. Rather than because they are old, it is because they offer an identifiable scenography that is well known. There the visitor-customer-inhabitant assumes a specific role, the place of a character in an appropriated memory. That appropriation can be for a short time or for a specific purpose, as in the case of leisure activities. No one really believes when visiting Disneyland that he or she is a sailor in the pirate crew in the Peter Pan saga, because in that case, according to the description by Phillip K. Dick, we could find ourselves more in a fantasy than in a fiction. Whereas the person who lives in a development built in the English style is more likely to go out wearing a Barbour jacket, drive a Jaguar, and take his children to an English school—an approximation which is closer to the building of a fresh reality in fiction, according to the aforementioned distinction.

3
Fictions in Architecture

Frozen Time

The urban planning rules of historical neighborhoods are an example of the weight of history. Priority is given to a type of architecture that existed in a specific period or age over architecture that could exist afterward. A regulation is created so that all new developments will fit into a prescribed model of architecture. However, there are always arguments when dealing with the sphere of maintenance work, as well as disagreements on whether the outside appearance only or the internal distribution, too, needs to be maintained to the standard of the past. Sometimes special considerations are extended for proposed projects and special by-laws are drawn up.

In all cases the characteristics of the desired model first have to be established. These characteristics have to meet two conditions. On the one hand, they have to have the potential to be dealt with objectively, be seeable, measurable and describable, in drawings and if possible in words. On the other, it has to be possible to fit them into regulations, to incorporate them into the rather tight confines of the limited framework, so that the technicians who will be supervising their compliance can apply them objectively and with a minimum of arbitrariness.

This forces an abstraction to be made of the chosen area of the city or the built elements. From the subjective interpretation of the pleasing appearance of an urban scene—mostly a sentiment that is widespread among citizens—it is necessary to move toward objectivization, and it is very likely that many essential parameters will be lost on the way. For example, in the case of the nineteenth-century expansions that are taken as the model of development, the composition of the block is made up of the sum of various properties, and one block was built by many owners and therefore by many architects, and so a different plan can be found for each house number of those groups of houses. By contrast, in a new neighborhood that has sprung up in recent years, more than one block has been built with a single plan. In this case the scale of intervention is the factor that remains in the selection process.

Paradoxically, the starting point for the selection or the decantation of the model is something "that cannot be named," a specific urban atmosphere which can be lost through the regulations given that the regulations can only cover aspects that can be named.

The reasons behind the selecting of a specific historical period or style for a new neighborhood can often differ. It could be that there is a particular neighborhood that simply receives broad approval and according to public opinion has best defined the desired ideals of the city, or that it has achieved the best result in the history of the area. These archictecural ideals are usually examples from the past, ones that have received favour and have passed the test of time, as opposed to new design proposels who's characteristics have not been tested or proven. As Nietzsche says, the creator is always at a disadvantage when faced with the monumental perspective of history.

In a number of cases, the town and city centers that designate Heritage sites become immersed in a "refurbishment" process. Following a period of unplanned development, all the elements start to be restored according to the model of a particular historical moment, and the distinguishing marks created in recent years, or even centuries earlier, are deleted. The aim of such a process is often driven by tourism, offering the visitor a scene of an age that can be found nowhere else. The city/town center starts to be filled with tourism services, and the ordinary activities of the citizens move elsewhere. An example of this is the town of Ainsa in Huesca (Spain). The heritage district is frozen in time, without any capacity to progress in time. The visitors find nothing there except other visitors. The main activity of the "protected" historical neighborhood turns into commerce, surrounding itself with services for tourists, immersing itself in an "endogamous circle." Here, too, the observer transforms the observed.

Another factor is the positioning of the collective memory, particularly in the neighborhoods and city centers that have already been built. The most radical cases are the reconstructions following wars. In such cases, the surviving population loses the context of its memories, and is driven to rebuild by the need to preserve historical identity. The urban scenographies that are fixed in the memory of individual and collective memories are retrieved, so that the memory of experiences may not be lost along with them.

Group memory and identity issues are linked to the preservation and recovery of built elements. Insofar as the city and architecture are the result of a specific cultural context, there is a wish to carry out the revival of that situation through the retrieval of them.

What seems clear following a war's slaughter, and within the course of the following generation becomes, or appears to become, more complex when it is viewed within a longer historical interval. Among these, the case of the city center of Berlin has stood out in recent years. It is one example that Ascensión Hernández Martínez deals with in her book *La Clonación Arquitectónica*, and it has received wide media coverage abroad because famous architects have participated in the debates.[1] A controversial issue was the rebuilding of the Stadtschloss. Located in East Berlin, it was severely damaged during the Second World War and subsequently demolished in the 1950s when a new City Hall was built in its place. The new building was a splendid example of modern orthodoxy. After it was built it became one of the main meeting centers for the citizens of Berlin. It became a prominent place in the memory of several generations, because it was the parliament building and because numerous cultural events were held there. The structure of the city center neighborhood was transformed, and a specific perspective of the old city was lost.

When Berlin was reunified, the wounds of the city began to heal, and the debate surrounding these places emerged. On the one hand, the new building had construction problems—it had been closed since 1990 because a lot of asbestos had been used in its construction and it was awaiting renovation work. Moreover, it was an obstacle in the way of the reconstruction of the prewar city

1. Hernández Martínez, *La Clonación Arquitectónica*.

structure. On the other hand, about forty years had elapsed since the Palast der Republik was built and by then it had been grafted onto the memory of those who live in Berlin today. However, the new version of the Stadtschloss that was being proposed was similar to the one before only in its external appearance; its promoters were proposing a program to adapt it to current needs, with offices, shopping centers, hotels and in general the things corresponding to a multi-use building of a city center. So what was in fact rebuilt was not the same building, but the urban scene it was part of.

Top:Berliner Dom und Spree-Ufer, 1945. Bottom: Palast der Republik, Berliner Dom und Spree-Ufer, 1985. Source: Slg Verfasser.

In 2002 the majority in the Bundestag adopted the following resolution: first, on the spot where the Stadtschloss had been previously located and blown up in 1950, and subsequently turned into the location of the Palast der Republik, a center devoted to non-European cultures should be built. The new building was to have the stereometry of the Prussian Stadtschloss and three out of its four Baroque façades and the Schlüterhof would be preserved. The architects would be given a free hand to arrange the fourth façade that would face the television tower. The Palast der Republik was pulled down between 2006 and 2008. The new building was named the Humboldt Forum, and in November 2008 the firm Francesco Stella Vicenza won the bid for the project. It is expected to be opened in 2015.

Here too, as on many other occasions, we are facing a Damnatio memoriae sequence. First, the communist authorities removed the traces of the monarchy that existed before the Nazis by demolishing the remains that were still standing in 1950. Recently, however, following the pulling down of the Berlin Wall, it is the remains of the communist regime that they wanted to remove. By removing public buildings and spaces they wanted to carry out a collective exercise in forgetting.

The Fiction of the Future

In the attempt to fixate architecture in a different time from the past, we also come across examples of going forward in time. In many instances this moving backward and forward in time has gotten mixed up, and has helped make predictions come true through the retrieval of past dreams, as in a *Terminator* film.

To prepare the set of the 1947 film *Metropolis*, Fritz Lang made use of the drawings of the futurist Italian architect Antonio Sant'Elia. By that time Sant'Elia was dead, but in his short life he left drawings that would become the precursors of future architecture. The very term Futurism indicated a "forward fiction" of time, as indicated by Marinetti's declaration, the desire to dismantle the traces of the past and move toward the future.[2]

These images have been turned into reality by the Marriott hotels of John Portman. The pictures below show how the images of

2. Marinetti, "The Founding and Manifesto of Futurism."

Antonio Sant'Elia "La Citta Nuova" (The New City), 1914. Source: Antonio Sant'Elia via Wikipedia Commons.

Left: Times Square Marriott. John Portman, architect. Source: Matthew G. Bisanz via Wikipedia Commons. Right: Marriott Marquis, Atlanta, Georgia, John Portman, architect. Source: dbking via Wikipedia Commons.

Ricardo Bofill, Les Espaces d'Abraxas, Marne la Vallée, Paris. Source: Ricardo Bofill Taller de Architectura.

Sant'Elia have been used to manifest an utopian sensibility that is meant to thrill tourists and travelers.

The obsolete photos in *Metropolis* have occupied a place in the collective imagination we have of the future and have been used as such.In the film Blade Runner the general perspectives of Los Angeles owe much to those street abysses among Lang's buildings. Nevertheless, to film the scenes in Blade Runner, what stands out is the fact that in addition to Wright's Ennis house and others, old film sets from Warner's black and white cinema were used. These were old sets that portrayed the streets of old New York used to film *The Maltese Falcon* (1941) and *The Big Sleep* (1946).

Even though the sets of Terry Gilliam's 1985 film *Brazil* are a combination of the above, cross-referencing *Metropolis* and Humphrey Bogart's films, has been called *retro futurism* and the very name is a testimony to the return trips made in time. Together with predictions made about the future or the past, one resorts to prediction to build an alternative to present time.

One of the locations used by Gilliam for his dystopia is Ricardo Bofill's *Les Espaces d'Abraxas* is in the city of Noisy-le-Grand in France. In a tangled paradox, a project using the language of classical architecture to build twentieth-century social housing using prefabricated industrial techniques is used to locate an imaginary nightmare that takes place in the future.

In the case of Stanley Kubrick's *2001: A Space Odyssey*, as far as the architecture of the film is concerned, it is a test of the predictions that were being made about the future at the moment it was shot in 1968. It displays the influence of Smithsons' "House of the Future of 1956," Eero Saarinen's furniture, the 1962 TWA building, and the space age collections of André Courrèges in the sphere of fashion. The reality of the years that followed took other paths, but now that we have reached the twenty-first century some of those aesthetics have been retrieved. The aesthetics of Apple products in recent years find their examples in the rounded whiteness of Mac computers, iPhones and iPods. Something similar happened in another field in those same years with the revival of André Courrèges garments at one time.

A Space Odyssey has become the aim of flashbacks, but the predictions of the future have ended up like a "Cosmicar," an old playground that has become obsolete. As the critic Michael Atkinson pointed out in his review of the film *Brazil*, Terry Gilliam realized that at the time when futuristic films were being made, they ended up being a naïve memory, and their success lay in turning that principle into a coherent comic aesthetic.

> Gilliam understood that all futuristic films end up quaintly evoking the naive past in which they were made, and turned the principle into a coherent comic aesthetic.[3]

Theme Architecture

As architectural models are a consequence of a cultural and historical situation, they are also converted into image-souvenirs to recall those situations, to use Bergson's term. The reverse side of that nature is the hope that through reconstruction they will once again embody the heritage preserved in them, the hope that, thanks to a reversal in the process, another period will be once again created and flourish around them as is seen in this passage from Gabriel García Márquez's *One Hundred Years of Solitude:*

> In all the houses keys to memorizable objects and feelings had been written. But the system demanded so much vigilance and moral strength that many succumbed to the spell of an imaginary reality, one invented by themselves, which was less practical for them but more comforting. Pilar Ternera was the one who contributed most to popularize that mystification when she conceived the trick of reading the past in cards as she had read the future before.[4]

This aim is not to be found in only one place, and as it is used to overcome time's frontiers of time, there is also a desire to break those of space. This has been a normal resource for changing the building types of another culture in one place. Each "colonization" has taken with it matching architecture and changes in urban-planning models, in the botanical sense of the word. Insofar as they have evolved into the universal indicator of Western Culture, these plantings have been carried out by force as well as in voluntary ways, and the model of classical architecture in the Greek and Ro-

3. Michael Atkinson, "Bravo New Worlds," *The Village Voice*, September 1, 1998.
4. García Márquez, *One Hundred Years of Solitude*, 49.

man case has spread all over the world.

But on a much more specific, more local, level architectural models have turned into the vehicles of total realities, in the way that universals could not do so for the very reason that they are universal. In this case what is sought is the repetition of a particular feature, the reflection of a specific context.

During the 2007–2008 academic year, two students[5] in the fourth year at the Faculty of Architecture carried out a study of the architecture of tourism in our Urban Planning workshop. This study monitored the models used over the years in Spain, urban planning and architecture linked to tourism, starting from the first developments in the 1960s on the shores of the Mediterranean up to the present day.

In the examples of the early years the scale of intervention was the building, a hotel or an apartment block. They were incorporated into the city structure and were attached to the public space that had not yet been built. One of the clearest examples of that model could be Benidorm, which maintains the ordinary urban structure even if its density has been taken to an extreme.

After that, the unit of intervention started to be the housing complex. Not only were buildings created, but also the private space around them was designed. In addition to hotels or apartments, many other services came together in the same block: restaurants, discos, bars, swimming pools and gardens. That housing estate resembled a neighborhood, and as it was located near a town that existed before it, it took the same name; it was a new neighborhood, but the tourists who stayed there had less and less contact with the original town. These units have become almost totally autonomous through the development of services, and instead of the tourists leaving the neighborhood, it is the local inhabitants who commute into these neighborhoods to work.

The next step has taken place in recent years during which the housing estate was converted from a neighborhood into a town. These housing units have become autonomous from the rest of the towns and new names have been thought up to identify them, names that are on the dividing line between toponymy and marketing. Brands have turned into the names of towns, in just the same way that what were once names of towns can be turned into brands.

5. Oihana Irazusta and Ismene Larringan.

On September 23, 2008, an item appeared in the press reporting that the Mango fashion outlet had signed an agreement with Barcelona City Council so that the word "Barcelona" could appear on the paper bags they give away in their retail outlets.

These resorts are no longer attached to a town, meaning a new entity has been invented. J. G. Ballard in his 1998 novel *Cocaine Nights* tells of what happens in one of them. He took a model resort, as used in some of his other novels, and depicted the nightmare that could arise when the development of its logic is taken to an extreme. Ballard's genre is science fiction and dystopia (the opposite of utopia), and *Cocaine Nights* is set in a resort called Estrella de Mar in eastern Spain. It is a little village where English people live, and they have hardly any relations with the surrounding Spanish people. They are retired people and their biggest problem is boredom. They have a group responsible for entertainments, which organizes games for them every day, but this is not enough. They need real events, and so the people responsible decide to organize a real murder.

Francisco Barba Corsini, architect. Binibeca, Menorca. Source: unknown.

In addition to the leisure services of some of these new creations exists the desire to create the illusion of visiting a different place, and credibility is sought as far as the tourist is concerned, so that on arrival he or she will find what he or she was expecting. Not unlike what Jack Pitman did in the novel *England*. In *England*, tourists seek a list of stereotypes which the average visitor might be familiar with beforehand, and this is what they build. These are theme towns, and the theme depends on a period or geographical location, mostly a kind of architecture that can be credible in that particular location. In Spain, they satisfy what a tourist would expect from their idea of Spain, whitewashed walls, wrought-iron grilles on the windows and stone floors; in Polynesia, stilt houses above the water; in the Alps, wooden buildings with steeply sloping roofs.

In Spain this is nothing new, and examples on different levels have arisen since the 1960s. One of the most successful examples is the town of Binibeca built in Menorca with the project of the architect Juan Barba Corsini. When it was built, it was regarded as quaint, even picturesque, but it turned out to be successful. It resembles a fishing village, and it respects the material and scale of the local village houses. In its structure and complements there are many elements that appear to be the result of chance. On the whole, as time passes it could pass for a traditional village.[6] This is what a tourist guide said in 2010: "It is a fishing village built in 1972. One might think that it is a theme park, but no, people live there and its silence must be preserved."

In the case of Pleta de Baqueira (Lleida), the neighborhood model was partly invented, through a re-working of elements taken from traditional buildings in the Aran valley (in Basque, haran means valley, so this is an appropriate example of the relationship between the name and the essence), and as a result of its success, it became an example of the authentic "Aranese" style of the valley consequently it is an example of a new model of a second nature having turned into a first nature.

In Andalusia, Benahavis, La Perla de la Heredia and La Heredia de Monte Mayor are other examples of this. The first is a town with a history going back centuries, and the new neighborhoods have taken its name. In the others, by contrast, it is difficult to distinguish between the commercial brand of a promotion and the town's name. On their web pages the adjective "picturesque" was not a term of contempt, but a positive marketing argument.

---

6. Juan Barba Corsini interview given to *El Pais* newspaper May 19, 2007.

La Perla de la Heredia, Malaga. Source: Unknown.

Seaside, Florida, as it appeared in The Truman Show, 1998.

Another step in this evolution process is taking place in several projects that have arisen around the New Urbanism trend in the United States. As in the examples of Orange County gathered by Edward W. Soja, theming has moved from the leisure parks to the sphere of homes, to neighborhoods where people buy their first homes.[7] The model established here is no longer a mere style of architecture. The features corresponding to built objects do no more than complement a whole environment. What is established here is a "model of life." They are closed communities—all the services are privatized, and the private aspects of life are also regulated so that they can be organized around certain values. Since the ethnic and economic diversity of the city began to be linked to the lack of security, some members of the economic middle classes have sought refuge in these new housing estates. They are prepared to swap some freedom and privacy for identification with a human group and the protection of a structured block.

One of the housing estates used for the 1998 film *The Truman Show* was Florida's Seaside, a model of what is known as New Urbanism.[8] The film is similar to Philip K. Dick's 1959 novel *Time Out of Joint*. The main character is Ragle Gumm, who becomes famous for continually winning a newspaper competition. One day an unusual detail attracts his attention, and he makes an automatic move to grasp a cord to turn on the light, but there is no cord there. From that point onward he starts to come across many cracks in his reality, until he realizes that he is a fictional character, and that, in actuality, lives in another year.[9] In the *Truman Show*, too, it is the little details that gradually warn the main character about the deception that he is experiencing.

Tourists experience a similar sensation when they visit certain "historical" towns, the spectator transforms the reality he or she observes, and when he or she leaves, the people remaining there will stop performing. When a fridge door closes, the light goes off, even though we always see it on, in actual fact the food spends most of its time in darkness just as Mickey Mouse and Peter Pan go backstage after a parade in a Disney park.

7. Soja, "Inside Exopolis," 94–99.
8. *The Truman Show*, directed by Peter Weir and written by Andrew Niccol, 1998. Seaside, FL, website, www.seasidefl.com, last accessed October 3, 2013.
9. Carrère, *I Am Alive and You Are Dead*, 39–44.

A forerunner of today's theme neighborhoods was what Marie-Antoinette ordered to be built at the Petit Trianon in Versailles. She ordered architects and landscape gardeners to build a fictional village around the main country house she owned. Real farmers were taken to live there and together with them horses, cows, hens, doves and lambs. The lambs had blue ribbons tied round their necks so that they could blend in with the bucolic atmosphere. From the inside, some of the farmhouses were elegant lounges for playing in. When the village was completed, the queen said it seemed too new and she ordered her workers to damage some things to make them credible.

In most of these projects where the fiction of an earlier time is built, an attempt is made to regain aspects that have been abandoned by rational projection. Among other things there are features of cities that have grown slowly as referred to by Camilo Sitte. How is it possible to create—in a city or neighborhood built as a single project in a short timeframe—the heterogeneities created by different interventions over the course of time, and by chance or as a result of criteria changes, and, in general, the exceptions that can emerge?[10] Considering again Borges's Gosse, how can glyptodont skeletons be created on the Luján gorge?

The solution is to invent that time, invent the passages as in a narration and to come up with a script that will tie them together. Sometimes these passages are real, and as Alan Berliner does in his documentaries, words and a new order are applied to them to make them credible.

One of these examples is the attempt made by Krier for the Benta Berri neighborhood of Donostia-San Sebastian. His project invented a type of structure of a historical European city. Linked to a vestige existing in the place and mostly invented, he created the scale, the geometry, the public space, and so on of a city center of another age.[11]

The new reality had a general look of belonging to another age, which helped it to be regarded as a dream, a fiction, and in this case, in line with Philip K. Dick's, closer to the sphere of fantasy. But the representation and chosen style hampered credibility in this case. The uniformity of the style of the project perhaps con-

10. Collins and Crasemann Collins, *Camillo Sitte.*
11. Moughtin and Shirley, *Urban Design: Green Dimensions*, 213–15.

tradicted the essence of the fiction of a long time having elapsed. But Krier's project did have some good aspects, and nowadays we can see them everywhere in journals and in totally different architectural languages; we can see similar features that attempted to revive those proposals, and which for a long time were regarded as picturesque in a pejorative way: divisions, misalignments, changes of scale, gaps, curves. Certain features that orthodox town planning has abandoned in some cases, are gaining strength in opposition to Hausmann's view. They have always been there in a kind of academic corner, but they are now meeting with popular success in Hondarribia, Binibeca or Seasides.

Iñaki Abalos says in his *Atlas Pintoresco* that when urban planning is done exclusively from the perspective of the plan, the perception of scale is lost, and that it comes close to the sphere of abstraction of "spatial planning."[12] Themes are one of the ways of protecting oneself against the results of that foreignness. But in the same way that a watch on a gladiator's wrist reminds us that we are in the cinema, the credibility of these architectures is limited. At one of these moments the cord to turn on the light does not work.

Here we could remember the answer given by Phillip K Dick in 1972 when a college student asked him to define reality: "Reality is that which, when you stop believing in it, doesn't go away":

> One day a college student in Canada asked me to define reality for her, for a paper she was writing for her philosophy class. She wanted a one-sentence answer. I thought about it and finally said, "Reality is that which, when you stop believing in it, doesn't go away." That's all I could come up with. That was back in 1972. Since then I haven't been able to define reality any more lucidly.[13]

The Evolution of the American Mall: From Victor Gruen's Inventions to Theme Malls

Theme architecture has taken the leap from closed leisure and entertainment parks to public and private spaces, and a good example

12. Abalos, *Atlas pintoresco*, vol.1: *El observatorio*.
13. Dick, "How to Build a Universe That Doesn't Fall Apart Two Days Later," 261.

of this can be seen in the evolution of the American mall. Following the Second World War, when neighborhoods modeled on the Levittown model were formed by low density, houses were repeated ad infinitum in the suburbs of cities in the United States. The large shopping center became the main meeting place for social life. Leisure and commercial activity came together in these malls, provided with large parking spaces for a dispersed population that got around by car.

The most repeated paradigm of that model was created by the architect Victor Gruen, when he turned the shop windows round to face the inside of the building, when he put retail outlets together on the upper floors, incorporated anchor retail outlets and in the middle created closed public squares. With its back to the surrounding car parks, it preserved within it a different isolated reality. The success of that model has lasted into the twentieth century since it emerged in 1956, and has spread all over the world.

But in recent years a new model has come about in the United States, and once again it is spreading all over the world: what we could call "theme" malls. The main feature of these new malls is the arrangement around open spaces, which are similar to traditional roads and squares. The Disney Parks or the "streets" created to look like nineteenth-century cities inside some Las Vegas casino are their nearest precursor.

The relationship that these new malls have with the surroundings is similar to that of the previous models, from outside they resemble large closed pavilions surrounded by car parks. When they are incorporated into the city, like The Grove in Los Angeles, the car parks are multi-storey buildings conjoined with the retail outlets. When they are in suburbs or sprawling cities, as in the case of Fashion Island owned by the Irvine Company in the city of Newport in Orange County, these car parks are never-ending asphalted surfaces surrounding the buildings. In both cases, the retail outlets face inward as in the previous model. The difference is to be found inside. This time what structures the shopper's route is a space resembling a street in the old quarter of a city. The interior façades of the pavilions are like those of the traditional type of building, brick bearing walls, wood carpentry, a repetition of the techniques and styles of building from the past. The street line is curved, in order to create numerous, limited perspectives, and the route is filled with little squares and expansion areas. In and between the buildings, fountains, terraces, platforms, ponds, gardens and many other items of furniture and built elements make up a heterogeneous, mixed block. In the case of The Grove, different styles of architecture are blended together: brick façades, Californian Art-Deco of the 1920s and 1930s, the colonial Spanish style, and the steel and glass decor of the Apple Center, too. In the case of Fashion Island, the style tends toward Tuscany, on the whole similar to all the closed new neighborhoods built all over Orange County and at Irvine Ranch in recent years.

Both examples make up a scenography like those built for cinema films, and the shopper is the main character. There is a show that takes place every day, like the daily celebration in Disneyland that incorporates the twice-daily carriage parade. Music can be heard constantly from hidden public address systems. At the Grove at Christmas they produce artificial snow from the roofs of the pavilions. In these two Californian examples this connection with filmmaking sources can somehow be regarded as intrinsically traditional.

In some of the retail outlets of these malls the building of fictions is taken to an even greater extreme. For example, at the Abercrombie and Fitch clothing shop, beautiful, unreal shop assistants—girls and boys who look as if they have just stepped out of a fashion magazine–wish shoppers a good morning. The boys do so with bare chests showing off their muscles, and the slender girls wear their best smiles. They are selected in castings like the ones done for films.[14] When I visited the store, two employees were standing at the entrance, right in the middle, the boy massaging a girl's arms, as if in a performance, without losing his smile. This fictional scene is made up of fictional characters, in the same way that Peter Pan can be seen walking past us in Disneyland. But while the latter is clear fantasy, the reality of the theme mall is approaching the limits of credibility. As Soja writes in "Inside Exopolis":

> Everyday life seems increasingly to have moved well beyond the simpler worlds of the artificial theme parks that you visit when you want to. The new theme parks now visit you, wherever you may be: the disappearance of the real is no longer revealingly concealed.[15]

---

14. See www.abercrombie.com/anf/careers/model.html, last accessed October 2, 2013.

15. Soja, "Inside Exopolis," 121.

At the entrance to The Grove there is a market made of wooden frames and little roofs, the Farmers Market, created by E. B. Gilmore in 1934.[16] It is full of boutiques and bistros. Seeing it together with the retail outlets next to it, it becomes impossible to know whether it is real or a "theme." According to the information, it was originally a place where the farmers sold their products directly and was a classical spot in the city. But one begins to doubt this when one sees it turned into a spot for leisure and curiosity shops are attached to a shopping center.

These new shopping centers have enjoyed tremendous social success. Their main feature is to create some identifiable urban scenes, which make shoppers feel comfortable, and which within a few hours will provide the atmosphere that one might find in a historical city.

The characteristics of these scenarios are beautifully described in the following passage by Christine Boyer. She classifies urban Tableaux, and distinguishes three types. The first includes historical neighborhoods protected by law. The second have special districts, urban scenes that make up strong, special perspectives. For example, she cites Union Square and Times Square in New York as protected by precise rules. The third consists of dormitory neighborhoods that have sprung up in many towns, commercial centers, "festival-markets,"and theme parks, the ones that have been skilfully "stage designed," with a planned decoration and atmosphere. She describes the last group thus:

> What characterize these new urban zones are the reiteration and recycling of already-known symbolic codes and historic forms to the point of cliché. Codes control signs, materials, colors, ornamentation, street furniture, and street walls; and codes also dictate the design of public spaces, the types of buildings, and the range of activities. Most important, codes contain a schema or program that generates a narrative pattern, a kind of memory device that draws associations and establishes relations between images and places, resemblances and meaning.[17]

This last sentence could be seeking the reasons for the success of

16. See www.farmersmarketla.com, last accessed October 2, 2013.
17. Boyer, "Cities for Sale," 188.

these scenographies: they create a model of narration, a memory device.

4
New Relatus

In the examples I have presented so far, in both the fields of architecture and in those outside of it, a credible past is built by means of a narration so that it can take the place of memories. The memories of the youth of the Nexus 7 android, the family memories of Felix Viscarret's dreamer, the rips and tears in the jeans manfactured by Jeanología, the nostalgia of theme parks and of little villages like Binibeca or Seaside, the wear and tear displayed by mock antique furniture, the 1930s façade of the mall. In the terms of Philip Henry Gosse, all these could be considered "prochronic" events, outside of time.

If one approves of the distinction drawn by Philip K. Dick, the hypothetical memories built through these contrivances are not fantasies, but fictions. They are credible and therein lies their success: they form a credible narration. In these relatus, on the one hand, locations are inserted into the equation, and on the other, the capacity that familiar images have to recall memories is successfully invoked.

All these buildings share common features in their compositions. On the one hand, they are made up of particular identifiable sequences. They bring together concrete events, or else their identifiable consequences, which have an objective physical reality such as photographs, tears, erosions, buildings, squares, parks, gardens. On the other hand, a line that confers unity on them ties them together like a thread, a material, a period, a route. And what is more, they are on the scale of the measure of the person, such that a person can feel them directly through proximity and through his or her senses. This whole is structured like a narration, which in this work I have named relatus, a word that can combine the meanings of narration and relation.

Recalling classical mnemonics, we can see that they have the same characteristics as those hypothetical buildings that were used for the exercises in rhetoric: places that were identifiable and distinguishable from each other, and an organization that enables a person to remember specific sequences made possible by passing through these places.

The Heterogeneity of the Historic City

It is no coincidence that the historic city is the most successful in the urban-relatus, and that Christine Boyer, for example, should put it in first place in her tableaux, or that the repetition of these parts of the city should be the most widespread subject in the area of theming.[1] One reason for this is its capacity for recalling a specific period in the past. But I do not believe that it is the main reason except in some specific cases. In the case of the exact postwar reconstructions, it could be the reason, because the inhabitants feel the need to retrieve the scenarios of their personal memories. But on the whole, for most of the population who has just arrived in the city, I believe there are other reasons.

In my view, they are related to what I referred to as the relatus structure, to scale, to heterogeneity and to the density of events. As Adam Caruso says in his work "The Emotional City":

> While one might intuitively be suspicious of the romantic variety and finely grained scale that now make the centers of our cities such popular tourist attractions, this consistent heterogeneity eloquently registers the mixed tenure and density of ownership and use so characteristic of and necessary to a liberal and democratic society. Hundreds of separate interests fronting onto a single street, all more or less subscribing to certain rules of engagement and benefiting from a multiplicity of social and economic transactions.[2]

A few lines further on he explains one of the main reasons for the lack that we notice nowadays, the change in scale that has taken

1. Boyer, "Cities for Sale," 187–89.
2. Caruso, "The Emotional City," 39.

place in the technical and economic process to build a city, whose symptoms can be the phenomena I have listed so far:

> While planning authorities may argue about façade materials and the survival of medieval street patterns in the master plan, several city blocks, that once housed thousands of tenants and were the ownership of hundreds, is now controlled by one owner backed by international financial institutions. . . . Rather than attempting to conceptualize the whole of urbanism, a critical architecture can emerge by ignoring the big and general and work with the minute and the highly specific. Architecture should be sensitive to those emotional qualities that define the city, melancholy, expectancy, pathos, hope. If one accepts that architecture is about altering and extending what is already there, one can engage the powerful presence of the real so that the aura of urbanity is amplified and extended in the place that one is working. The complexity and interconnectedness of the city is sustained by such instances of profound invention.[3]

So we could take complexity and interconnectedness as the characteristic of a way of doing architecture that pays attention to the particularities.

Competence to Build

The evolution that the concept "heritage" has undergone can provide us with another enlightening perspective along the path to theming. Françoise Choay makes a stark diagnosis of today's situation in *The Invention of the Historic Monument* while conducting a historical monitoring of the concept "heritage." According to the analysis she has done, the term "heritage," on the one hand, has reached increasingly broader realities, from designating certain public buildings, to covering whole towns and cities, construction techniques, and natural ecosystems, celebrations, festivals, gastronomy and many other realms. On the other hand, the ubiquity of tourism has also jeopardized the very survival of the notion of heritage. Since the demand is much greater than the supply, cultures have started to build replicas. The criteria for designating something as a "heritage site," together with the expansion of such sites,

3. Ibid., 39–40.

means they lose their specificity, and frequently the only objective criterion is mere antiquity.[4]

When analyzing the current situation, Choay sets the moment for change in the 1950s. Up until then, tools represented technical human activity, and through them the "humanizing" of the world. But by the second half of the twentieth century, with the revolution in transport and electronics, the relationship between human beings and their physical environment has been turned completely upside down. Distances have been wiped out, links with respect to the local context broken, and instantaneousness has replaced the continuity of time. When physical distances are removed, tourists and vegetables move from one continent to another, thus removing the frontiers of geography and the seasons. The compression of time could also have caused memories, questioning, waiting, and coming-and-going times to disappear. The consequence of that disappearance of links with respect to local time and spaces is the destabilization of identity.

The lack of time could be the origin of the simulations of time I referred to above. If the time for scuffing shoes disappears, they are bought already scuffed.

The consequence of all this in the sphere of town planning is the destructuring of the traditional town or city by creating "network town/city planning," where an isotropic urbanization spreads all over the land like an urban nebula. Another consequence, the opposite of the above, is the disappearance of articulated structures or fabrics and the contexts. On the scale of buildings, on the other hand, scant attention is paid to integrating them with the nearby environment.[5]

In Choay's view, the only way of getting out of that pessimistic reality is to retrieve the "competence to build," somehow to base oneself on history but to retrieve the competence to create new realities.[6] In that seeking of memory, the most productive way would be to, once again, achieve the competence for creating memories.

Yet the difficulty in such an initiative would lie in the resources. Insofar as the intellectual tools and projections that have led us to

---

4. Choay, *The Invention of the Historic Monument*, especially chapter 6 "Historic Heritage and the Contemporary Culture Industry."
5. Ibid.
6. Ibid., 164–78.

this situation have failed, the ways of creating new projects would have to be invented. The evolution that has taken place in cultural heritage over the past half a century is a symptom of a failure. It has come along to fill or conceal that gap which has been left by that failure. This, means, in Choay's view, a loss of the power over organic time that such momuments had. This power, an ancestral relationship of the continuity of time, has been, since then, the object of desire that is experienced as absence and loss.

The competence to build would have an anthropogenetic function and Choay represents this through two representations of Western culture. First, the myth of Daedalus, because his labyrinth would be "the human building par excellence: the one that can capture the continuity of time and oblige space to delay its deployment, so it can head toward the sense." Secondly, Ruskin's proposal which at the time was calling for the creation again of a "historical" architecture to challenge the architecture that was being done in his time, in other words, to go on creating history. In addition to criticizing his contemporaries, he also denounced the copy of past forms. When he criticized the pastiche, what he was denouncing was the obstacles placed in the way of "organic" memory by the "artificial" memory established by the history of art.

> And when he condemns pastiche and the reproduction of past forms, Ruskin thereby denounces the obstacle riased before organic memory by the artificial memory of forms instituted by history and corroborated by historical monuments: an obstacle even more real in our time and concerning which the perspicacious Viollet-le-Duc had already declared surmountable only by a deliberate practice of forgetting, in the course of a strenuous dialectic of memory and history.[7]

Choay defines the "competence to build" thus:

> Our capacity to articulate among themselves and with their content, through the mediation of the human body, the elements, positive or negative, solitary but never autonomous, whose deployment on the earth's surface and in the course of duration generates meaning, both for the one who builds and for the one who inhabits the buildings, just as the deployment of the signs of language in acoustic space and in the course of

---

7. Ibid., 176.

> duration signifies both for the one who speaks and indissolubly for the one who listens.[8]

We would have to acknowledge heritage's propadeutic task, insofar as it teaches us scales, proportions, articulations, contextualizations, the duration of side roads or circuits. But the aim should no longer be its blind preservation, but to retain the competence to produce a continuation and substitution of it, so that in the future it can also be our memory.

In the field of architecture, as in many other fields, one argument for breaking with the past was the proclamation of individual creativity, we could turn here to the following words in T. S. Elliot's essay "Tradition and the Individual Talent":

> What happens when a new work of art is created is something that happens simultaneously to all the works of art which preceded it. The existing monuments form an ideal order among themselves, which is modified by the introduction of the new (the really new) work of art among them. The existing order is complete before the new work arrives; for order to persist after the supervention of novelty, the whole existing order must be, if ever so slightly, altered; and so the relations, proportions, values of each work of art toward the whole are readjusted; and this is conformity between the old and the new.[9]

Spaces Imbued with Quality: Heterotopias

The structure of the elaborations that we are examining could therefore consist of two types of elements: events on the one hand, and the thread that joins them together, on the other. These events are singularities of space, places having distinguishable qualities.

The concept heterotopia described by Michel Foucault appropriately describes the most radical manifestation of these places that have their own quality.

According to Foucault, we are experiencing an era of space, of simultaneity, of juxtaposition, of proximity and distance, of coexistence and dispersion. In his view, our world of today, rather than

8. Ibid., 172.
9. Eliot, *The Sacred Wood*, 49–50.

developing like a life through time, appears in the form of a network that connects points and interweaves its own skein. This spatial aspect that appears on the horizon of our system is not an innovation, however—space has a history in the Western experience, and it is not possible to disregard this interweaving of time and space.[10]

When providing a brief history of space, he starts from the Middle Ages. The medieval space would be a group of places that was organized according to a hierarchy, the espace de localization. After that, with Galileo, the space became open and unlimited, that which is open and without limits. In the Middle Ages, the place occupied by a thing dissolves and becomes no more than a dot in its movement, and its rest is no more than the slowing down of the movement. From the seventeenth century onward that "localization" was to be substituted by "extensiveness."

That "extensiveness" would be substituted today by "site." Site is defined by relations of vicinity between points or elements, and these relations can be described as series, trees or networks. Our epoch is one in which space assumes for us the form of relations among sites, and "time" would only be another option in the possible relations.

That space is sanctified. As phenomenologists have shown, we do not live in a homogeneous and empty space, but on the contrary, it is imbued with qualities and perhaps under the spell of invention as well. Therefore we do not live in an empty space. We live inside a set of relations that delineates sites which are incompatible with each other, "we live inside a set of relations that delineates sites which are irreducible to one another and absolutely not superimposable on one another."[11]

All the sites could be defined by means of the relations between them, but among them are some that have a curious property of being in relation with all the other sites, but in such a way as to somehow, separate, neutralize or invert the relations that they express or reflect. Despite being related to all the other sites, these spaces contradict them all and are of two types. Firstly, there are utopias, sites with no real place, unreal ones. Secondly, "heterotopias," real places, utopias that have somehow been realized, created by human institutions but separate from other places and which are found in specific places. Between the two there is a mixed experience: the mirror, on

10. Foucault, "Of Other Spaces, Heterotopias."
11. Ibid.

the one hand shows a space that is not real, but at the same time the mirror itself exists.

Heterotopias are "counter-places" that are created by all cultures. He calls the science that undertakes to describe these places "heterotopology," and he lists and describes its six principles.

In his lecture "Les Hétérotopies" broadcasted by France-Culture station on December 7, 1966, Michel Foucault uses an example taken out of everydayness to explain the nature of heterotopias, in other words, the behavior of children. He says that children naturally distinguish between these heterotopias or "counter-places." One example of this would be the hut at the bottom of the garden, the garrett, or even more so the teepee set up in the middle of the loft, or the parents' large bed on Thursday afternoonwhere the sheets can represent the sea, the sky or a hiding place in the forest.

This concept of heterotopia is used by Demetri Porphyrios to define the plurality of places in Aalto's works, setting it up against the homotopia of the orthodoxy of the modern project.[12] Taking Foucault's terminology, Porhyrios cites two categories underpinning the sensibility of heterotopia: discriminatio and convenientia. Discriminatio is the classifying of things according to their differences. Convenientia refers to the arrangement of different things next to each other, organized spatially in a non-stable unity.

The Structure of the Relatus

Behind all these structures, those that can be perceived in a fuzzy way are constructions built piece by piece, new juxtapositions are made with elements imbued with different meanings. Their structure is heterogeneous and the relations between them are temporal and spatial. The organization of the whole that they comprise is that of a narrative, a narrative structure, which is of that which is known as *relato* in Spanish. The term *relato* derives from the Latin *relatus*, and literally means "taken back" or "related." The definition of the Spanish word "relato" provided by Wikipedia can shed light on this: "The story is a discursive structure, characterized by narrative heterogeneity, and in the body of the same story different types of discourses can appear."[13]

12. Porphyrios, "Heterotopía."
13. Translated from Wikipedia entry for "relato": http://es.wikipedia.org/wiki/Relato (last accessed March 20, 2014). Original reads, "El

This way of building the wholes applied to architecture would be that which is inferred from different proposed or reflections gathered here. What does not produce a complete structure lays emphasis on specific spots that are decisive for development and which have to be completed with the beholder's intelligence. Its structure is discursive, made up of heterogeneity and different types of buildings can appear within the same whole.

Heterodox Modern Architecture

Even though architctural themes and the inflation of heritage are largely the consequence of town planning carried out in the twentieth century, there have been creators in these years who have come up with a coherent narrative structural proposal from the techniques and functions of their time. In the sphere of unique constructions, constructivism may have been the most powerful, collective attempt. An attempt was made to create a new "second nature" with the resources of a new era. A participant in a revolutionary political project, it was the architectural component of the project of a new society. Nevertheless, beyond the scale of the buildings in the area of town planning, along the line of a trend toward monumentalism around collectiveness, its results were not very different from those produced by modern orthodoxy.

From the positions that were critical of the orthodoxy of the modern movement, there have been numerous attempts that should be taken into account. For example, the new network of pedestrian space that was proposed for the center of London with the Smithsons' project for The Economist. But the most robust proposals came from those which were capable of creating formal open systems that had the capacity to respond adequately in the same spot to each different scale. Among them I would cite the names of two masters in particular: Alvar Aalto and Hans Scharoun. The Seinäjoki town center or the Berlin library, respectively, are examples of the excellent results that have been achieved with the personal tools that each of them developed.

In *The Other Tradition of Modern Architecture*, Colin St. John Wilson puts those who, led by Le Corbusier, established the modern or-

---

relato es una estructura discursiva, caracterizada por la heterogeneidad narrativa, y en el cuerpo de un mismo relato pueden aparecer diferentes tipos de discurso."

thodoxy from the CIAM, up against Alvar Aalto, Hugo Häring, and Hans Scharoun, in particular. In the passages in which he describes the features of what he called "the other tradition" appear those of the narrative structure or the one structured by the relatus that I am describing in this work:

> Combinations of these spatial figures form a narrative that is the real art of architecture. And it will be in this medium of charged spatial experience that the masters f the Other Tradition have worked, rather than in the refinement of an object and its "forms in light."
>
> What we are therefore offered is a narrative of event and episode where movement, pause and coming to rest are paced in direct response to the activities that the building was built to serve, with something of the precision and the propriety of a rite, yet performed not with the aura and sacred repetition of ritual itself, but the spontaneity of a living pursuit—the unselfconscious participation in a seemingly natural choreography.
>
> By the same token, the breakdown in scale from large to subsidiary forms will be made not so much by stressing the mode of structural assembly (as, for instance, in Kahn's claim that there is enough decoration in the marks of a building's construction), nor by the game of proportional composition on planar surfaces (as in Le Corbusier's traces régulateurs), but rather by the elements that respond to human presence and touch (a rubbing-strake, a dado, a handrail, built-in furniture and fittings), the intimate language of inhabitation.
>
> We are therefore concerned with a way of working that sees a building not as an object to be contemplated from without but to be entered, experienced within, used.[14]

Through this work I would like to relate the work of Frank Gehry to the work of the aforementioned two, and present him as the creator of narrations, which on the basis of contemporary tools constitute an alternative to fiction.

Zeigarnik Effect: The Memorability of Incomplete Narration

In the theory of psychology there is a phenomenon that has to do with the structures we have been analyzing, with the breaking up of incompleteness, the Zeigarnik effect. According to this principle,

14. St. John Wilson, *The Other Tradition of Modern Architecture*, 108.

we remember unfinished tasks better than the ones we have completed. This tendency is based on the motivation we have to carry out tasks, and from the parts we are prompted to imagine the whole, to mentally build the structure made up of pieces that we perceive. As the architect and professor Santiago de Molina pointed out in a text he wrote on the Zeigarnik Effect, "all the fragments that are already outside our view are ordered, but only at the moment in which their sequencing stops. This shows that for architecture to be moving, some kind of rhythm has to be developed between the user's body, perceptions and memory."

Examples that Display the Traces of Time: English Football Grounds

To understand what the relatus structure consists of in buildings, I propose that we look at football stadiums to seek examples, because they clearly show the formal consequences of the time factor. Football grounds are public buildings, today's equivalent of the circuses of the Roman Empire, and the unforgettable events that take place in them are retained by the fans in their memory linked to the scenario. And they are also monuments inside the city, buildings that become a reference, premises for social events and, because of their size and scale, the town/city boundaries of the neighborhoods where they are located.

Although they are built according to the same program–a rectangular grass field to play on, surrounded by stands for the spectators–depending on the relationship they have with time, we can, on the whole, distinguish two types: the ones that have been developing and changing over the years, and the ones that are planned and built in a simple shape at a specific moment.

According to the theory I am proposing in this work, the first would be the ones that create the structure of the relatus as they are. In them the stadium itself is not a single unit, each of the elements that are created around the field has a distinct nature. Normally a stand is built on each of the four sides, while in stadiums that are gradually built piece by piece over time, the stands have been built in different periods. As the number of spectators grew in such cases, or depending on the needs of the time, they were extended or renovated. The result is not an identifiable geometry. They are hetero-

Villa Park, 1907

Villa Park, 1966

Craven Cottage, Fulham, London. Source: Nigel Cox via Wikipedia

Craven Cottage, Fulham, London. Source: author.

geneous blocks made up of different parts. Inside them they bring together the elements of different techniques, epochs, builders and types. What provides them with unity is the square of the pitch, the scene. Let us consider some examples.

London's Craven Cottage: It is located in the suburb of Hammersmith and Fulham, next to Bishop's Park, on the banks of the River Thames. It has been the headquarters of Fulham F.C. since 1896. The first stand was built according to the plan of the Scottish architect Archibald Leitch in 1905, together with the house beside it called the Cottage. This stand was known by the name of the Stevenage Road Stand until 2005, when to mark its centenary it was given a new name. That year Johnny Haynes, a much loved former player of the Fulham fans and a former captain of the England team was killed in an accident, and the oldest part of the stadium was named after him, the Johnny Haynes Stand. Today both the Cottage and the stand have been designated heritage sites.

The side facing the river, Riverside terracing, was famous because from there the fans were able to watch The Boat Race (the rowing race between Oxford and Cambridge). The new stand known as the Eric Miller Stand was completed in 1972. Today it is known as the Riverside Stand.

Between 2002 and 2004 Fulham had to play on another pitch, because the stadium did not meet the minimum safety requirements. During the 2004–2005 season, the new stands were completed behind the gates of the pitch, Hammersmith End (Hammy) and Putney End.

Recent years have seen endeavours to have a new, larger stadium built somewhere else, but because of the wishes of the fans these plans were dropped, and a decision was taken to gradually increase the capacity with small improvements every year over each summer.

The Cottage building on the corner had been built to house the changing rooms. Relatives of the players used to watch the match from its balcony and today tickets for it are sold as special tickets. Its volume is similar to that of the houses in the neighborhood, its red brick façade provides a continuation with the Johnny Haynes Stand, and as one approaches from Finlay Street it finishes off the street perspective and articulates the scale of the stadium with the structure of the residential houses in the area.

The fans have known this football ground by many different names: The (River) Cottage, The Fortress (or Fortress Fulham),

Thameside, The Friendly Confines, SW6, Lord of the Banks, The House of Hope, The Pavilion of Perfection, The 'True' Fulham Palace and The Palatial Home. The River Thames that passes on one side is called 'Old Father' or 'The River of Dreams.'

Anfield stadium was built in Liverpool in 1884, also with the plan of Archibald Leitch. The names of the four stands: Spion Kop ("the Kop", 1906), Main Stand (1895, 1973), Centenary Stand (previously Kemlyn Road, 1963) and Anfield Road (1903). The name Spion Kop was taken from a mountain in South Africa, where three hundred British soldiers, most of whom hailed from Liverpool, were killed while gaining a battle position during the 1900 Boer War. In 1928 the Kop was renovated, and throughout England many stadium stands have also adopted the name Kop. In 1982 the gates known as the Shankly Gates were opened in memory of the former manager Bill Shankly. Above them are the words "You'll never walk alone," the title of a song by Gerry & the Pacemakers that was a popular hit in the 1960s and which has since become the anthem of the Liverpool fans.

A curious example of attachment to a place is that of the Stamford Bridge pitch used by the Chelsea Football Club. As a result of financial problems in the 1970s and 1980s the Chelsea Pitch Owners not-for-profit organization was set up and today it owns the club's name and pitch. It restricted voting rights to one hundred shares whatever the percentage of ownership might be so that it would not end up in the hands of property developers. Stamford Bridge is the stadium with the smallest capacity among the top Premier League clubs and the chance to build a larger stadium elsewhere has often been mentioned. But this plan faces an insurmountable obstacle: in the articles of association of Chelsea Pitch Owners it is stipulated that should the club ever leave Stamford Bridge, it would not be allowed to retain the name.

All these issues could be of limited interest from a merely architectural perspective, but the key is that they have remained "written" in the buildings, and they exert a direct influence on the shape the buildings assume. Due to the manner in which these architectural projects slowly developed, these buildings have another lesson for us. As a result of being created in bits, they grow in bits. As time passes, what was there before is gradually adapted through transformation but without being made to disappear completely. As they have not been created according to canonical geometry, and as a result of not seeking the monumentalism which that geometry could signify, they have had no problem being sewn together in an unorthodox way. They have been able to gather together bits of buildings of different dimensions and uses, and they have often formed heterogeneous blocks. St. James Park in Newcastle-upon-Tyne is one of the most striking examples of the consequences of the various opportunities and difficulties that have arisen in the course of time. Attempts to extend this stadium have come up against obstacles because of the building and infrastructure surrounding it. This has resulted in the square formed by two different pairs of L-shaped stands, with one of the L-shapes being considerably higher than the other. The shape is not at all canonical, and the uppermost seats apparently afford splendid views of the city.

Each section of these building blocks keeps its name, which is the vestige of a particular, intrinsic memory. A specific group of fans sits in each stand. The memories of each spectator are linked to the specific location he or she had in the stadium, spatial references are not ordinary points that exist in a single geometry, but, very much to the contrary, specific places that have their own uniqueness. Behind the name of these elements is hidden a specific nature. This naming of parts is the most enlightening reflection of the autonomy of elements that make up the block. The incorporation of time opens up the opportunity to mythologize the space. The structure of space produced bit by bit coincides with the structure of time, with a sequence of happenings, which is where happenings and memories leave their trace. A new toponymy is created with the naming of parts that make up the stadiums, in the same way that names are assumed by the topographical peculiarities in a geographical area. The last section of this work will be devoted to seeing how in Frank Gehry's projection process, too, the custom of naming parts emerges as the symptom or consequence of these formal characteristics.

There are other kinds of stadiums, most likely the majority, which are totally different from the stadiums that have been built bit by bit in the course of time. They are the ones that have come about and been completed in one single production. Most of those being built today, the Emirates Stadium (of London Arsenal), the Allianz Arena (in Munich), the Stade de France (in Paris), Bei-

Anfield Road, Liverpool. Source: Ben Sutherland via Wikipedia Commons.

Stamford Bridge, Chelsea, London. Source: www.wallfootballclubs.org.

St. James Park, Newcastle. Source: Sir-Nobby via Wikipedia Commons.

St. James Park, Newcastle. Source: www.apiedepista.es.

jing's Olympic Stadium, and many more, are of that type. These have been built and completed from a single plan, and they have a single identifiable geometrical image as their formal starting point and aim: oval, circular, elliptic. In them, the stands have no beginnings or endings, because they are continuous rings. The seat of one spectator is distinguished from another only by the position with respect to the pitch. They hardly develop through time, because the opportunity to expand does not tend to be included in the program of projects. To be renovated, they would have to be renovated completely. Without going too far afield, we have right here the difficulties encountered by the project to renovate the Anoeta stadium in Donostia-San Sebastian, among other things because of its roof is one unit. It is not possible to change, remove or add to a part of it without affecting the whole, in the same way that it is not possible to remove the keystone from an arch. They were built at a specific moment and bear the traces of that moment; rather than the traces of the passing of time they bear witness to a historical moment.

Such prominent stadiums are created for a historic event in many cases—to host the Olympic games, world cup football championships or similar—and they also fulfil a symbolic function. Such an aim pushes projects toward monumentalism, and in this task the most effective ones are those with a single geometrical shape and which can be identified, shapes that can be identified at a glance and shapes that beyond direct perspective can provide strong images in the media,as well. Thus the hanging ring of the Stade de France, the "bird's nest" of Beijing or in Munich, the structure of the Allianz Arena resembling an inflated blue or red coloured cloth. This seeking of simplicity moreover, leads to the building of abstract objects devoid of scale, which, forgetting their nearby surroundings, has more to do with models on the scale of the whole country or of merchandizing. In such cases what we come across surrounding the stadium is a plot of land, a piece of land that has been emptied out in advance so that the new object can be placed in it. The abstraction of the object to be built calls for the abstraction of the place in advance. Names, too, in some cases, have taken the path of abstraction; the trend has changed from using names that were once used to identify the place, the toponyms, to using others linking them with international companies, like Emirates Airlines or Allianz.

Emirates Stadium, London. Source: Repin, at www.skyscrapercity.com.

Allianz Arena, Munich. Source: www.taringa.net.

With respect to the program, today's trend is to gather inside the stadium what at one time originated in the neighborhood. In the past, pubs, restaurants and shops used to be dispersed among the contiguous neighborhoods. When there was a championship or competition in the stadium, the celebration spread and was reflected in all the surroundings. The spectators used to meet in the surrounding pubs before and afterward, and the retail outlets also used to benefit from that proximity. In the new model, these added economic activities have turned into a significant chapter in the profitability of the economic exploitation of the stadium itself and have moved into the interior of the building. An example of this is the Emirates Stadium of the Arsenal Football Club in London, which has replaced Highbury since 2006. There, what are not toilets are bars all along the perimeter that leads to the stands, it is full of screens where the spectators can spend their time while they wait. The middle, smaller and more select stand has a direct link with a smart restaurant. In other words, the isolation process is not just formal, it is also social. When the building like a balloon releases the strings attached to its surroundings, it releases them in all aspects. In these isolated positions new objects turn into elements for admiration, in other words, the symbols of an organization or State that can be identified and repeated for media purposes.

Frank Gehry's Work: An Example of the Construction of New Narrations

One of clearest examples in the last twenty years of architecture having a narrative structure is that of Frank Gehry. During the post-modern era, when there was a desire to revive the city's human scale and memory by means of the impossible and mostly sterile repetition of historical models, Gehry, on the basis of building systems and forms of his time and context, was able to come up with a new model. In his projects, rather than being single buildings, he proposes a contemporary way of "creating" the city, paying attention to the surroundings in each case, with the sensibility learnt from art in the 1960s, but using the intrinsic tools of architecture in a professional way.

It is evident that his attitude with respect to post-modernism is critical, and he makes it clear with a touch of irony when he speaks about the creation of his "fish." At a time when the post-modernists proclaimed the need to look back, he said "OK, if you have to look back, fish were around three hundred thousand years before human beings, so why don't you go back to the fish?" Even though we could have doubts as to whether this reasoning was the starting point or was a later reflection, the sentence shows Gehry's position with respect to post-modernism: his wish to explore freer rules outside its restricted confines.

The project he did between 1988 and 1992 at the Paris Euro-Disney shows more clearly than in any of his projects the divergence between these two attitudes, and at the same time the similarity of aims. Disneyland is a paradigm of theme architecture, and more than the park itself the leisure neighborhoods built around it also reflect thematic architecture. What stands out in the park is the distance with respect to reality. Anyone who visits Snow White's castle, the far-west town, Dumbo's circus, or Alice's maze, sees them with sufficient distance, except for the children who believe that Mickey is real. But in the resorts arranged around it the distance is not so great, and the visitor who gets immersed in it can end up being a participant in a role play.

In this context the Gehry building is the only one without a theme, but at the same time it had the formal elements to turn it into a theme. The interpretations of this clash appear in the following story of his:

> Euro-Disney is a maverick in my work. I think the thing I did wrong there was not doing the interiors and all the Mickey Mouse stuff. I said, "I can't do that." But I think I would have made the building come off if I had done it. It would be a consistent thing. I didn't realize that I could become themed, but I was. . . . Mine was the only building without a literal theme. Everybody at Disney loved what I was doing. There are two things I don't like. One is that if you have seen everything else, my building becomes a theme in itself, because it's the only one out there. It's a de facto theme. They put restaurants in my building, and stores, and themes galore. And they asked me to do them. They said, "Why don't you do them—the 50s diner and all that stuff?" I said, "I'll do them my way, but not themes.[15]

15. Friedman, *Gehry Talks*.

In an article on Frank Gehry written by Alejandro Zaera, the author highlights the attempt to create that "second nature" based on an anthropological sense in Gehry, and the audacity to build a representation system that could be an alternative to pure simulation. This is what he said in one section:

> The work of Gehry must be considered as a last attempt to maintain the possibility of a "representation" of reality, just before this possibility disappears in the paradigm of "simulation": an eseential slackening of the anchorage of the signifier , with the hope that a widening of representational systems will permit the possibility of an architecture that is not completely "simulated", where the "sign" can still maintain some value. Just as we have seen, Gehry's strategies have been fundamentally directed to the implication of the subject in the experience of the architecture", an implication that is not limited to a purely formal, spatial or material experience of the architectural objexto, but that attempts to include realities external to its pure objecthood. Ghery's work invades the domains of the "significant", both in the field of the symbolic and the re-presented, as in the directrly sensual. The architecture of a "secondary naturalism" cannot simply base itself on the "constitution" of the object; it must at the same time contemplate its anthropological meaning. In the absence of a valid representational system within the traditional discipline of architecture that can confront unmeasurable realities, Gehry returns to analogic, magic or mythic thought: the fish and the serpent as well as the "Lockheed 101" belong to a mythology that is in part personal, in part tribal, "totemic", with which Gehry can confront the resemantization of everyday reality."[16]

In the next chapter I will examine three of Frank Gehry's projects, taking Alvar Aalto as the forerunner in some aspects.

16. Zaera, Alejandro, "Frank O. Gehry, Still Life" in *Frank Gehry, 1987–2003*, 53.

5
Frank Gehry's Three Projects

> It is not what a building looks like on the day it is opened but what it is like thirty years later that matters.
> —Alvar Aalto

Most of the world's major cities have an image that identifies them; Paris has the Eiffel Tower, London, Big Ben or Tower Bridge, Berlin, the Brandenburg Gate, New York, the Statue of Liberty, Washington the Capitol. These images have turned into the symbol of the cities and a sign of a city trademark. But in the case of Los Angeles there is nothing that has assumed this role. There is no city perspective or specific building that is a symbol representing the whole city. The huge letters of Hollywood are the closest to fulfilling that function, but rather than a specific place they remind one of a host of fictions. Nevertheless, when we visit it, everything strikes us as familiar, and despite not identifying concrete elements, the atmosphere is familiar to us or else we feel that we are inside a film. As Jean Baudrillard said, you don't find Los Angeles cinema at MGM or Disneyland, but in the streets, "marvellous, continuous performance of films and scenarios. . . . It is not the least of America's charms that . . . the whole country is cinematic."[1] Cinema could be, together with the freeway, the symbol of Los Angeles.

Baudrillard is right describing the perception of an European when arriving to Los Angeles, the evidence that he has reached the west limit, the familiarity of this urban landacape never visited but so many times sawn in films and the limitless:

> Dawn in Los Angeles, coming up over the Hollywood hills. You get the distinct feeling that the sun only touched Europe lightly on its way to rising properly here, above this plane ge-

1. Baudrillard, *America*, 56.

> ometry where its light is still that brand new light on the edge of the desert. Long-stemmed palm trees, swaying in front of the electric billboard, the only vertical signs in this two-dimensional world.
>
> At 6 a.m. a man is already telephoning from a public phone box in Beverly Terrace. The neon signs of the night are going out as th3e daytime ones become visible. The light everywhere reveals and illuminates the absence of architecture. This is what gives the city its beauty, this city that is so intimate and warm, whatever anyone says of it: the fact is it is in love with its limitless horizontality, as New York may be with its verticality.[2]

Rather than a city, Los Angeles is like a country unto itself, in view of its size, distinctive culture and way of life. Homogeneity prevails, an isotropic structure that only stops when it reaches the ocean or the surrounding mountain ranges. The only breaks from horizontal references are the urban centers rising up in the middle of the landscape, and they, too, belong more to the geographical scale than to the sphere of urban elements. Frank Gehry says it is "the chaotic product of democracy," without an architecture that "holds us," a beautiful city without order based on the automobile and free democracy, the place where each citizen holds his or her own rights, and that is what is reflected by its architecture and buildings:

> For me LA has been in the front line of that kind of chaotic product of democracy. We do not have any historical architecture to ground us or hold us—I will not say hold us back, because I do not think it needs to hold you back. LA is a pretty messy town built on the automobile and on freewheeling democracy, where everybody has their own rights and the architecture and the buildings reflect this.[3]

There is a sentence in this text that is more than a physical description and which is directly related to some points in the thread of this work, "because I do not think it needs to hold you back." In this sentence it is possible to understand implicitly "I think it needs

2. Baudrillard, *America*, 52.

3. Jencks, Charles. 1995. Gehry, Frank. "Since I'm so Democratic I accept Conformists." In "*Frank O. Gehry: Individual Imagination and Cultural Conservatism*." Academy Editions. 40.

to hold you," that there would be a need for these built references, but they do not have to be a link with the past.

In the midst of this sameness large tracts of the country are organized without references as in a web, and as Gehry says, without an architecture that holds them, and his three urban projects that I will be analyzing here have arisen out of these conditions. They are three projects that put into practice the strategies for creating new narrations or relatus. They are different in their programs, but in them he has used similar resources to isolate them from the context and create precincts in which a fresh distinct reality is created.

The first is a small museum connected with the subject of the sea, the second a small shopping center, and the third a group of buildings belonging to a Law School, a kind of small campus.

The surroundings, in the three cases, are places that do not offer a specific reference for pedestrians, and in the three the strategy of the project is to offer a public space of a closer scale. These new places are made up of different parts, they are diverse in terms of shapes and materials, and each one offers a route made up of a sequence of small units.

These three projects are a demonstration of an approach, built in the same city within a few years of each other, and which display the use of similar strategies and formal tools. That provides sufficient unity to be the object of a joint analysis and to be an example of the proposal presented in this work. Moreover, the fact that they are located in Los Angeles somehow confers the nature of a laboratory experiment on them, like an experiment conducted "in vitro." As Rafael Moneo said "Being contextual in Los Angeles means ignoring the context."[4]

Cabrillo Marine Aquarium, San Pedro

"A lifeguard showing kids shells on a table" is how Ed Mastro, the exhibits director of the Cabrillo Marine Aquarium, describes the institution's origin. And this is not mere rhetoric, this is the guiding spirit that it has always had and that it maintains[5]. Bob Foster was the name of that lifeguard who in the 1920s worked on Venice

4. Rafael Moneo, "Reflexiones a propósito de dos salas de conciertos (Gehry Versus Venturi)." Walter Gropius Lecture. Graduate School of Design, Harvard University, April 1990.
5. Conversation with Ed Mastro on January 20, 2010.

beach and used to set up a card table beside his lifeguard tower to exhibit shells. His hobby was to collect different kinds of shells on the beach, and then he would give explanations about them to anyone who approached, mainly children.

Cabrillo beach was built in 1927 by means of a dike, and when the Olympic Games were held in Los Angeles in 1932, the sailing races took place there. For that purpose a new building was built, a boat house. Three years later, in 1935, Bob Foster's collections were taken there and that building became the first headquarters of the Cabrillo Marine Aquarium.

Bob Foster's place was taken by another lifeguard called John Olguin. In the 1950s and 1960s he set up "beach programs" and "grunion programs." There, school children as well as adults got to know the local sea fauna and flora. The grunion fish lays its eggs in the sand during the neap tides, and then the males come along and fertilize them. Two weeks later the young grunion are washed out to sea with the next neap tide. One of John Olguin's activities was to organize night excursions to see those fish disembark on dry land. It has to be said that the sea environment around Los Angeles constitutes a very rich ecosystem. It is the spot where cold water currents making their way down from the north meet the hot southerly ones and create unique conditions.

As a result of the success of his programs, the old 1932 boat house was starting to get too cramped, and in the 1970s the City of Los Angeles Recreation and Parks Department embarked on a project for a new building. It was initially thought that it could be located on the beach itself, close to the visitors, but because of the influence it could have on the natural environment another location had to be sought.

The inland side of a car park next to a hill further away from the beach but within reach of the visitors was chosen. In the new location the building lost its direct contact with the beach and the sea, and as an architectural project its nearest environment and reference was the large, flat asphalted surface of the car park.

Susanne Lawrenz-Miller, a doctor in biology, was appointed to carry out the project for the new aquarium. And together with John Olguin, a working team was set up that would run the institution over the years to come. Frank Gehry was appointed to draw up the plan.

Cabrillo Aquarium's metallic frame during 1974 construction.
Source: Cabillo Museum

Susanne Lawrenz-Miller and John Olguin with the aquarium plan.
Source: Cabillo Museum

They wanted to have some live marine animals in the new building, but without losing the spirit that had existed until that moment, in other words, making the visitors part of a piece of research. The responsibility for the work was divided between Sussane and John, the former as the researcher and the latter as the teacher. These roles were clearly reflected in the project, Sussane's office facing inside has the features of an open laboratory, and John's, facing the beach beside the visitor's reception, is next to the auditorium.

The aim of the new building was not to create an artificial reconstruction of the natural reality, but a place to explain that reality. Ed Mastro uses the word "flexible" over and over again to describe it, "notices are pinned up with drawing pins and not put in a frame, so that they can be changed at any moment." He also uses the word "campus," denoting an open area. People can enter free of charge, and beachgoers can come and go as they please.

Regarding the materials used by Frank Gehry and the formal features of the building, they evoke local references: first, they reference the industrial buildings of the port of San Pedro beside it, and secondly the structures used at one time to hang the fish so that they would dry.

Ed also remembers an argument that arose when metal fences were put up, because of the aesthetic drawbacks and the risk that the plastic fish hung from them would fall. The argument they used to keep them was apparently a totally pratical one: they formed a security fence in the event of burglaries to which such an open building could be vulnerable.

The exhibition does not proscribe a specific route, the geometry of the route is deliberately complex and the visitor can make different choices for his or her approach to the exhinit, "exploration" being the word used to describe what the visitors do. At 10 a.m. a yellow school bus arrives at the gate and a group of children and teachers arrive. They are the only visitors until twelve noon when the doors open to everyone. They moment they arrive a group of volunteers welcomes them and divides them up into small groups without any specific order in different spots in the installations. These volunteers are indispensable in the Cabrillo Marine Aquarium's organization; they number about four hundred, mostly retired men and women and they undertake to provide the children with all kinds of explanations. A similar approach was used by Gehry in 1980 in the Los Angeles Children's Museum project.[6] There, too, many exhibition rooms were linked by a network of ramps and staircases, and hands-on exhibitions for children were organized. The block resembled a city. Frank Gehry himself participated in the programming of several exhibitions and activities. His wish to organize such work experiences with the children dated back to the 1960s. At that time he helped his sister Doreen Nelson with the programs sponsored by the Smithsonian with inner-city children. In those workshops the children analyzed the city and used the models as reference points to get to know the city and make new proposals. In Gehry's words, through this work, the children had to learn to criticize the activities of adults by asking questions and having their own opinions. This activity must have been enjoyable for them, and must have been useful for linking the planning and design with enjoyable experiences, "because you remember easily what is good and enjoyable."

The route followed by the visitors to Cabrillo is made up of variable elements that are separate from the main structure. There is a corridor, which is of a complex geometry and which has unspecified directions, but which can be followed from inside as well as outside, and the path that needs to be taken is not specified in advance. From inside, the tanks can be seen through a kind of window, but from outside all the pipes are visible like most of the elements in the building's installations. If you choose to go through the inside of the corridor, you come across the perspectives of an ordinary aquarium, the fish and plants are behind a window, but if you opt to go outside, you become immersed in the technical side of the set-up. The technicians do their work among the visitors and even when there is a barrier for safety, there are windows which allow the work to go on in full view of everyone.

In the exhibition area Gehry used an unusual flooring technique so that the installations could be changed. The whole surface of the floor is made up of concrete paving stones laid on sand, and whenever an alteration or repair has to be made to the pipes passing underneath, all that needs to be done is to lift them up, do the repairs and the put them back in their place. It is a solution that also works well for drainage purposes. "Flexibility!" says Ed Mastro

---

6. Germano Celant. "Frank Gehry: Buildings and Projects" Children's Museum. Rizzoli: New York, 1985.

once again, with a touch of pride, when he gives his explanations. We should say flexibility and lack of specification of the activity. As Louis Kahn used to say that the seed of a library was "a reader next to the window," here one could say that it is "a child going into a laboratory asking questions," or "a lifeguard showing the children the shells he has found and displayed on a table."To avoid the need for an air-conditioning system and at the same time allow natural light into the inside of the building, there is a large skylight above the exhibition and some smaller ones above the laboratories. They open by means of motors to achieve cross ventilation from the doors.

Strategy with Respect to the Cabrillo Marine Aquarium Site

As you approach by car you come across the CMA building at the end of a low density neighborhood not far from the port. As you go down a slope to get there, what first strikes you is a large car park next to a beach and beyond that, next to it, a small, modest building. (In 2004, in view of the success of the Aquarium, an extension was built with a project by the firm of architects Baron Phelps & Associates, but for the purposes of this analysis the original will be analyzed.) The building is located behind the car park, nestling in the slope, on one side of an endlessness breadth which starts from the car park and the beach and heads seaward.

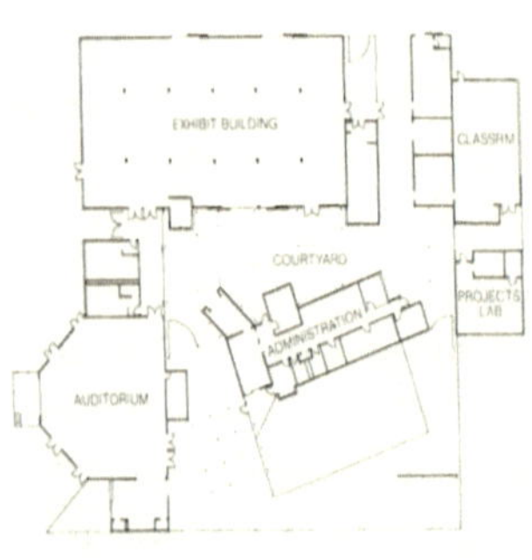

Cabrillo site plan and aerial view

This page: Views of Cabrillo Marine Aquarium. Photos by the author.

In this context, the first gesture of the whole is to form a U-shape, a fence that retains within it a restricted space. This U-shape has its back to the slope and from the car park opens out to whoever approaches. At that opening at the mouth of the U-shape, another building is placed like a wedge; it is small, somewhat smaller than the main buildings that delimit the precincts, and conceals the inside but without shutting it off completely.

This element leaves two gaps on each side, a wider one on the left as you approach, and a narrower one on the right, and controls the flows toward the inside like a valve. Many hints are created to announce that the door is on the broader side: the left arm of the U-shape is longer, it is closer to the car park, and the end of the volume of that arm is broken to announce the first door of the auditorium; the wedge element is also curved, it is not in line with the main building, and that way the "mouth" on the left-hand side is further forward with respect to the one on the right; the metal structure shaping the interior scenography protrudes as far as the sidewalk; and finally, so as not to leave any room for doubt, there is a free standing wall that conceals the door on the right at the front of the block with the name of the building.

As a result of the two accesses formed by the pavilion that closes the U-shape, the interior space is not arranged according to a single, static axis, but according to a route, and the path taken by the visitor when he or she enters does not finish at a specific point of the building, but provides the option of going on and turning back toward the outside. That way the arrangement of the elements comprising the block is not completely hierarchical, but is according to a route. On that route, options on another level are also gradually created: a passage that leads to the car park located on one side of the building, the one that provides access with the services elements located behind, and between the two main buildings—the auditorium and exhibit building—the door that provides access to the services space on the left. (This latter passage was used by Phelps to connect with their extension.)

The empty internal space ends up separate from its surroundings, autonomous, a covered structure made up of galvanized steel tubes and metal webs. Toy fish hang from it, somehow wanting to play with the illusion of being immersed in the sea. The scale of the car park, the beach and the port have ended up far away, and a new reality has been invented.

Edgemar, Santa Monica

In 1908, the Imperial Ice Company had a 750 square meter warehouse built with a bow-truss ceiling and clerestory windows behind a plot of land located in the high street of Santa Monica. In 1928, another structure was added onto the previous one. In the 1940s, because of the decline in the ice business brought about by the development of refrigerators, the minority shareholders, the Michel brothers, purchased it for the egg-processing section of their dairy shop and added a small building in the art deco style on the high street side to house their offices. The warehouse built in 1908 was turned into a room where the eggs were held up to the light to check whether they had been fertilized.

At the same time they ran a competition in the newspapers to find a name for their company, and the winner was "Edgemar," made up of the English word "edge" and the Spanish word "mar" (sea).

In 1983, the Michel Brothers moved and put their Main Street property on the market. The following year it was bought up by the neighbour Abby Sher. Frank Gehry was commissioned to produce the plan for today's Edgemar and they asked him to keep the existing buildings. The artist Thomas Eatherton was familiar with the main building of the warehouse and he suggested to Abby Sher that an art center be set up there. As a result, the two of them with a small group of friends, founded the the nonprofit Santa Monica Museum of Art (SMMOA). In February 1985, they obtained permission from the municipal council to create a multi-use block there, which in addition to the art center, was to have shops for rent, offices and a restaurant. In 1988 its first art exhibition was inaugurated. In 1994 the SMMOA moved its headquarters and in 2003 the Edgemar Center for the Arts, devoted to drama and the performing arts, opened in the 1908 warehouse.

It is in a well-to-do neighborhood surrounded by low-rise houses. Here too, as in the whole city, people get around by car and there are few public spaces on the scale of pedestrians apart from the sidewalks.

Michael Sorkin links the Edgemar project as well as the other two we are indirectly analyzing, with a tradition "to make places"

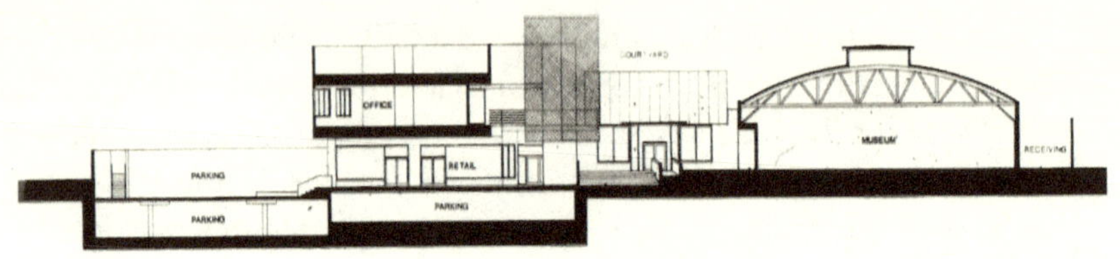

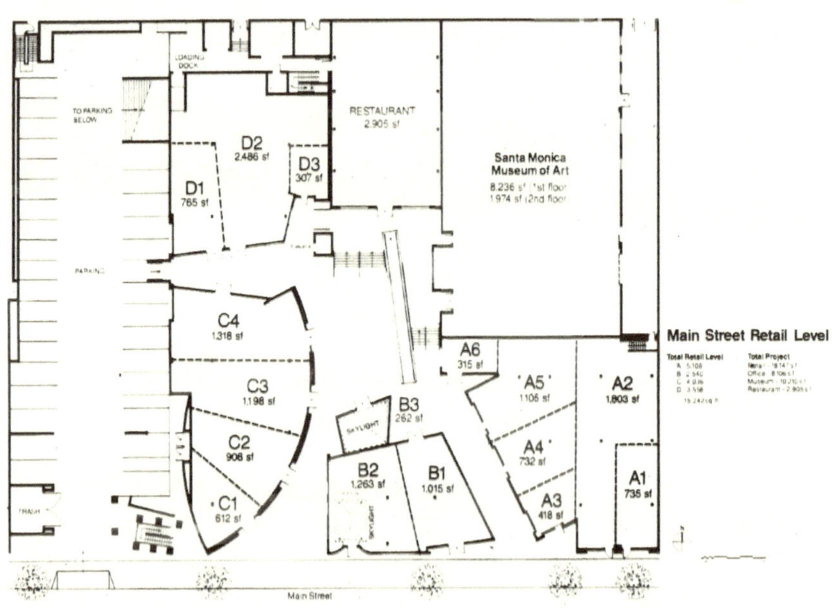

Edgemar plans, courtesy of Gehry Parters, LLC

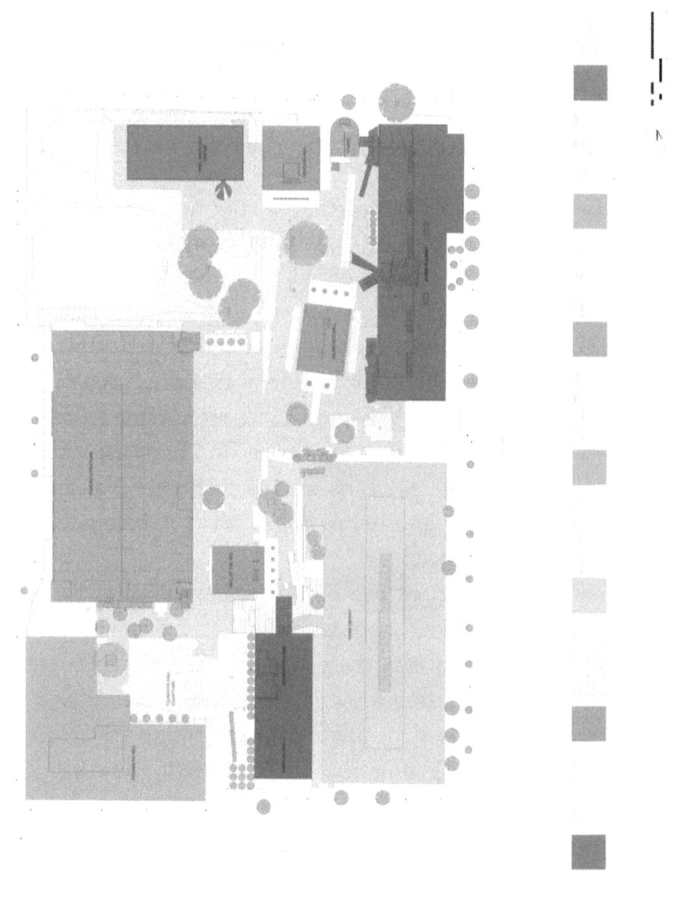

Loyola Law School plans, courtesy of Gehry Parters, LLC

in Los Angeles:

> The bringing together of pieces in peaceable assembly is the most urgent creative agenda of Gehry's breakout. . . . Slighted in this interpretation are certain sounder elements, especially a history of local place making. The film studio complexes, endearing shopping centers, like the Farmers Market, bungalow courts, and especially the small pedestrian cul-de-sacs, such as the Crossroads of the World, are clear prototypes for the likes of Edgemar, one of Gehry's most successful ensembles.[7]

Strategy with Respect to the Edgemar Site

In this context the Edgemar Center uses the same strategy seen in Cabrillo. The open part of the U-shape opens out onto the street, and the functional closing off of it is produced by a part with a trapezoidal foot. The remaining two gaps are of equal value here, there is no main entrance, and consequently the transversal direction is emphasized. The lower floor of this small center comprises, in addition to the ECA, a shop, café, restaurant, hairdressers and various commercial outlets. On the second floor there are offices to let. Outside the main precincts on one side there is a car park. From there, as at Cabrillo, another passage creates a third public entrance into the interior space.

The external part of the building that delimits the main precincts is ordinary, like that of Cabrillo. Some ordinary windows appear in its composition in the places required by their function, and the surface is built using cement and painted. Yet inside it is totally different and forms a complete attrezzo by means of a confusing morass of different geometries and materials. The sheer volume of the building blends with many other elements that do not appear to have any functionality. Some elements, having been raised above the cornices of the building, appear to be there to attract the attention of drivers, in an attempt to break with the monotony of the high street and express the uniqueness of the place. Others are hanging from structures to compensate for the narrowness of the interior space, reducing the height of the interior space where the café terrace and the passage between the shops are located. The

7. Sorkin, *Some Assembly Required*, 101–2.

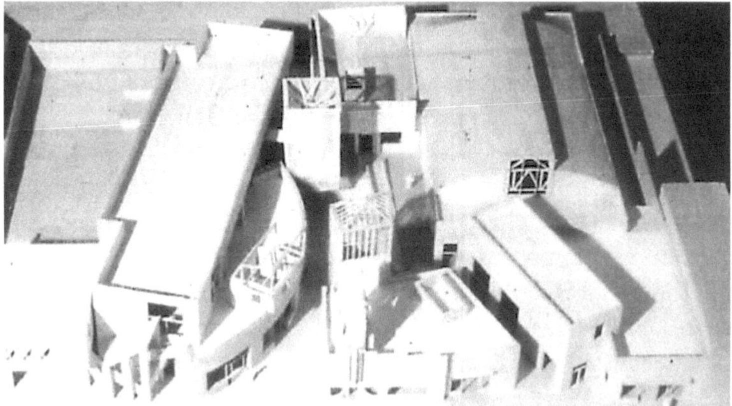

Edgemar model. Model by Benjamin Marcus.

block looks as if it has emerged in a random way. There is no clearly prominent order or structure, but all the things that appear seem to contribute to a specific atmosphere and scale.

In the case of Edgemar the components of the interior space form an attrezzo, without any specific theme, but with the effect of creating an appropriate spatial scale and ranking. Functionally, they provide an entrance square to the exhibition halls and theaters which have been created in the old warehouses. The building that is to have the main public function is offered an open space like that of a small village square, but it escapes from monumentalism and avoids excessive hierarchy, in a complex space where retail outlets, leisure activities and routes are tied up with each other.

Loyola Law School, Los Angeles

The Loyola Law School (LLS) founded in 1920 moved in 1964 to a plot in the Pico-Union district, where is it located today. In the early years it had a single building, which today houses the William M. Rains library. In 1973 it merged with Marymount College.

It is by the downtown area of Los Angeles, on Olympic Boulevard. Its surroundings are made up of ordinary commercial buildings and mediocre housing. It is regarded as a dangerous neighborhood to frequent.

In 1980, with the intention of organizing the LLS's expansion needs around a nucleus that would have its own identity, Frank Gehry was called. The result is a campus, delimited by a group of buildings making up a fence to protect it from the outside environment. Its structure, and the iconographic references of certain elements comprising it are reminiscent of the agora or forum.

The main feature of the program is that it is broken up into constituent parts. In the published explanation given by the,the author, economic reasons for doing the project this way include Separating those uses that required larger structural spaces—thus allowing for the optimization of structure and cutting of costs.

Through this decision, each building adapts to a specific type of space, and the diversity of uses is directly reflected in a diversity of built volumes.

In the project, as in most of Gehry's works at that time, geometric complexity lay in what was not built. The complicating of a spatial experience is achieved through the complex juxtaposition of single elements that have a modest, light structure.

Strategy with Respect to the Loyola Law School Site

As seen on previous occasions, here, too, the perimeter of the plot is made up of buildings that display their most neutral aspect to the outside and a double entrance is located on the open side of a U-shape. Here, too, the access from the car park forms the third entrance. The position that was occupied by the administration building at Cabrillo or the little art deco pavilion at Edgemar is taken here by the chapel, leaving one entrance on each side. One of the two gaps is considerably bigger and has an entrance staircase. On the other, a narrow ramp meets the accessibility requirements. As in Cabrillo, the element located in the middle has its back to the outside, and it emerges on the outside as an abstract façade volume and copper roof, concealing its true scale and responding appropriately to the rawness of the street.

So that the imbalance between the widths of the two entrances does not stand out too much, one immediately comes up against the emergency staircase that comes down from the lecture room building. With a formal prominence that is not justified by its function, it interrupts the main axis that had started to form part of the entrance staircase. If one turns round and looks back, the tower of the chapel anticipates the tower structure that was to be built at the Bilbao Guggenheim on the other side of the Salve bridge. What in Bilbao is a steel structure that is half exposed and half covered with stone is here more modest and has a wooden structure and copper cladding. As in the volume of the chapel, it emerges as an abstract prism from the exterior and shows its true skeleton inward.

From the entrance onward there are continual doublings of the routes, interruptions and diversions. To achieve this he uses little buildings of different sizes, and other elements as well: benches, trees, the main staircase up to the lecture room building, level changes. Although the administration building opposite the entrance initially adopts a different position in the hierarchy, the route for reaching it is divided up, as if wanting to balance the dominance of the building with the narrow access, and what is more, the way does not end there, because through a final swerve it reaches a space like the last open "cloister."

The surroundings of the Loyola Law School are stark. It is in the middle of a ring of services created around it by the city's business center fortress, and on a lower level. Most of the surrounding buildings are warehouses, car parks, industrial plants, hotels or old apartment blocks. There is no neighborhood life, let alone public spaces for pedestrians. It is the most deprived part of the city, the starkest, a kind of non-place. In the midst of all this, rises up the "wall" made up of the faculty buildings. They present sturdy boundaries, to which all the others are added and aligned in the perimeter of the block which existed previously without any kind of adornment on the outside. What stands out more than anything is the total contrast between the façades that face inward and outward of the Casassa, Burns, Donovan Hall and Girardi Advocacy Center buildings. While the inside ones are distinguished from each other with bright colours inside the block, the surfaces facing outside display a striking ordinary quality and have been finished in a rough, grey base coat. Inside the campus each of the buildings claims its own individuality, but from the outside they emerge like a "fence" closing off the block.

Inside, a new pedestrian space is being created. The headquarters of the various student organizations that are underneath the lecture room building fulfil the function of retail outlets in a public square. The small rise of the awning protecting it renders the scale change with respect to the outside clear.

Since it was built the block has undergone a significant change because of the building of a new car park. It is the most important volume among those that make up the complex, it is more separate from the middle than the previous one, and as a result, the internal space has become wider. Through a level change the trace of the original limit can still be picked out, the internal space has not been distorted, but the new surface that has been gained is almost totally empty, and stands out significantly from all the rest, without managing to become integrated into the general arrangement.

Nevertheless, some people have drawn attention to the pessimistic view of that boundedness, or fortification tendency. For example, in "Fortress Los Angeles," Mike Davis takes these strategies to delimit and isolate an area as an example of the privatization of public space caused by capitalism and driven by an obsession about security, and in the LLS in particular, so much so that Frank Gehry was given the nickname "Dirty Harry" in one version of the work "Fortress L.A."[8]

When one sees the surroundings, the measures to protect the necessary scale and atmosphere required by the academic activity appear indispensable. It is true that driven by security needs, what used to be the main entrance in the plan of the project is today closed, and the car park has ended up as the only entrance. This has somehow transformed the success of the strategy that we are analyzing.

The Strategies that Are Repeated in the Three Projects

There are some strategies that we can find repeated at the three projects here analyzed. And the similarity in their projectual tools are indeed the main reason that they have been selected for more detailed explication in this work.

The Delimitation of Precincts

The strategy adopted in these three projects start by establishing the limits of the precincts. In all three the first gesture and the first step is to create an enclosure. The buildings form a barrier that will

8. Davis, "Fortress Los Angeles," 155–57. Gehry and LLS are discussed specifically at 167–69. Davis uses the nickname "Dirty Harry" in another work, the chapter "Fortress L.A." in *City of Quartz*, 236–40.

establish and delimit the ambit of the project.

In the case of Cabrillo there is not even any street structure, a plot of land in the corner of a car park is chosen and the building itself delimits the space for work, and differentiates it from the adjacent endlessness of the beach. The plot of Edgemar is fixed, but it is like many others, yet another plot in a structure made up of homes and warehouses. The preexisting building of the Loyola Law School was an isolated volume, incorporated into the stark area of the land surrounding the downtown area. The surroundings in the three cases are according to the scale of the car, without any pedestrian-sized public spaces.

In the three initial projects delimitation is carried out through the continuous and austere fence buildings. In the first, these buildings are new and are U-shaped. In the case of Edgemar and Loyola, preexisting buildings are incorporated into this function, and the position they occupy on the edge of the plot ends up complemented with new buildings.

In each case these new limits create a new, identifiable unit, which will thereafter end up completely separated from the surroundings. The interior spaces created are public spaces on the human scale, and unlike previous ones, offer a new identifiable place and a space for new activities: a sea aquarium, commerce and leisure, and the law faculty campus, respectively.

In the open sections of the three U-shapes that are the starting point he adds a smaller element by way of stopper or spigot in the three projects. They are places between the arms of the U-shapes and an entrance that is left on the two sides. In Cabrillo, by means of a U-turn, he establishes a hierarchy between the two, because the running of the museum calls for the establishing of a main entrance. In Loyola, one has a staircase and the other a ramp to meet accessibility requirements. At Edgemar the two match each other.

The doubling of the entrance is indispensable to enable the interior route to be organized dynamically. A single entrance would have caused an axis to be created, but the fact that there are two creates a moment of ambiguity, which opens the door to a diversity of routes. Moreover, that way of entering prevents the immediate interpretation of the space: it delays the process of full understanding, and adds a decisive time factor. The visitor does not understand the interior as a single space, but as a sequence of time and space.

Instead of being one single place, it becomes a complex made up of many individual places. These identifying places make up a spatial relatus brimming with the rhythms of the routes. In this narrative structure the visitor then goes on to form the telling of his or her particular experience.

Once the external conditions have been left behind, the development of the internal spaces is in accordance with the new reality. Even though the perimeter buildings respond to the scale of the surroundings, the components that appear inside are on a smaller scale, and have a closer interpretation. The routes are shorter, different formal events start to appear in the rhythm of the route for pedestrians, and that act of walking is an irregular continuity of different sequences. Guidelines are not needed any more, and the visitor's choice of passages is expanded. They are public spaces that fit the user, and citizens can appropriate them.

One of the principal features of Frank Gehry's way of working is the dividing up of the program, that is, as he says, the first decision in the project. That way each part can be given the formal response that suits it best. As a result, the blocks produced are made up of identifiable parts, and that helps the time sequences to appear in the general structure.

In these projects, in addition to the component parts of the program, other built elements also appear. They could appear gratuitous from the perspective of a limited understanding of functionality, but they have their use in adapting the features of the new interior space and in the formation of the new relatus. They serve to interrupt and measure the continuity of space, and on other occasions they open up the possibility of a new level of interpretation.

Establishing a *Temenos*: The Greek Model According to R. D. Martienssen

In R. D. Martienssen's 1968 analysis of Greek architecture, he puts the basis of the space-idea of the Greeks' acropolis in the strategy established by the limits of precincts.[9] In the preface to his work, Martienssen provides a critical interpretation of the analyses made of Greek art. In his view, most of the analyses of Greek art has been done from archaeological perspectives alone, most likely out

9. Martienssen, *The Idea of Space in Greek Architecture*.

of necessity. The objective of these analyses is the direct analysis of objects, and they were not far removed from the literalness of the discoveries. They have focused on the analysis of remains that have survived to this day, and mostly they have not taken the step toward trying to find and understand the spatial concepts prevailing over these specific works.[10]

Views based on aesthetic judgements would have ended up outside the scope of the work that has been kept within such a narrow mold, for fear of falling into the field of partisan theories. As a result of this he perceives a need for a general understanding of the Greek system, which would go beyond the sole perspective of the discipline of archaeology and which would be studied from other specializations. His essay is written from the sphere of architecture, from different scales, starting with the creation, location and arrangement of cities right up to the structuring of the house.

Martienssen takes his work to those broad areas, quoting Professor Rhys Carpenter:

> The new school should not treat anything as isolated or separate, it seeks to fit every fragment in its place, hoping to piece together a general unity, wherein as it were a individual human eye, hand and intelligence can penetrate thousands of years of effort and creation through it. . . . Its aim is not to accumulate but to understand.[11]

After analyzing the location and arrangement of Greek cities and the house, he becomes immersed in the analysis of the temple and the "temenos" in the last section of his work, and he bases his theoretical proposal on the interpretation he makes of them. We can draw analogies from the analysis of the complex that is arranged around the temple.

The complex that is created around the temple is the acropolis, and its first component is a flat surface. Although this surface, the one at Epidaurus, for example, is arranged on a single level, others, like the one at Sinium, are made up of many horizontal planes. That first basis establishes the concrete reality of the physical place and the relationship it has with the topography and landscape of the land, and it will confer a unity on the complex that is made up of

10. Ibid., xiv–xv.
11. Ibid., xiv.

numerous elements around the temple:

> A horizontal plane, or a series of related horizontal planes, is the first essential in any system if formal arrangement intended to embrace the activities of organized or collective life.
>
> In historic times, as we shall see later, the paved terrace was an integral part of the Doric temple setting, and, indeed, contributed largely to the plastic unity of the separate but relates elements that constituted the temenos or enclosure.[12]

So, the whole arrangement carried out on that surface base should be understood as a single whole. The buildings and other kinds of commemorative monuments that are gathered together in the acropolis are the components of a catalogue that is repeated in the examples that were built over many centuries in the lands of ancient Greece.

As the temple and the altar were essential among these elements, they were put together with others, like the propylaea, the stoas, the tholoi, the statues or the lesser temples to form a complex inside the temenos. They do not all appear in all cases. At the acropolis in Delphi, for example, there is no propylaeum, or in the case of the Epidaurus a tholos and a stoa appear, unlike in most of the six cases studied. But all of them would basically follow one and the same system, according to Martienssen. The essence of the system there would not lie in the features of the particular elements, or in their number, even though they, too, form a coherent whole, but in the relations that are created among these related volumes. And these relations are not static ones, they are not univocal, but diverse ones. This system is made up of the different relationships which the spectator, the visitor, encounters, insofar as he or she is a walker. The buildings enclose the volumes that measure and establish internal space, and the traveler, when he or she approaches them and wanders among them, while he or she moves in the gaps, establishes his or her own position through their positions.

> Although we are assuming that the spectator is within the boundaries of the system, it can be shown that the relationship is not one-way in character, but offers significant attributes also when the spectator is outside the physical limits of the system. . . .

12. Ibid., 3, 4.

This other quality that Martienssen finds at the Greek acropolis has to do with the shortcomings of many views that have spread about Frank Gehry's work:

> One should not read any isolated significance into these elements; they are not "features" in themselves. Only in their balanced synthesis does the essential effect emerge.[13]

Frequently, exclusive attention is paid to specific buildings, or to put it another way, to the materiality of the built objects. As a result of getting too close, what could be perceived from a broader perspective is not seen. The materiality of the buildings, being powerful and striking, has concealed the sense that the projects have as a whole. This aspect has intensified as the geometries andof the shapes of Gehry's repertoire have become more complex, including the use of "more brilliant" materials.

Going back to Martienssen, one of the features, and perhaps the main one, in the arrangement of the Greek acropolis is the order based on the movement of a traveller wandering around it. These arrangements have little to do with the more rigid systems that have subsequently been developed throughout history. That has often prompted modern historians to hold contradicting views on the lack of a closed alignment or order. It has been taken as the consequence of a hypothetical lack of maturity of ancient Greek art in some cases, or as the consequence of the lack of a project that would have arranged the complex in its entirety. In the case of the acropolis (as cited by Martienssen) the British architect and archaeologist Francis Penrose asserted the following:

> This lack of exact symmetry is productive of great beauty and exquisite variety of light and shade.[14]

Pierre Lavedan, the French urban planning historian, suspected a lack of arrangement:

> The buildings, taken by themselves, are beautifully and rationally constructed. The ensemble, however, is a confused accumulation of altars, temples, statues, and lack both the

13. Ibid., 7 (first quote), and 47 (second).
14. Ibid., 112. Cites Martin L. D'ooge, *The Acropolis of Athens* (New York: Macmillan, 1909), 113, where the Penrose citation is unattributed.

> necessary distance to judge the beauty of each, as well as the subordination of the various parts to the whole.[15].

Martienssen's theory, of course, concurs with the first one. When he analyzes the sanctuary of Asclepios at Epidaurus, he analyzes the location, which is lacking in any kind of alignment, of the propylaeum, the temple, the tholos, and the stoa that form the whole, and this is what he says:

> Analysis discloses a constant measurement between the adjacent buildings in this list. . . . In view of the lack of alignment between these buildings, this strong positional identification within the temenos suggests a form of co-ordination that has its basis in a space continuum of advanced type. The "order of co-existing elements" is such that each building is profoundly significant as a volume, and any position taken by a spectator within the scheme tends towards three-dimensional conception of all these volumes.
>
> The articulation of elements results in a rich interplay of separate entities whose visual possibilities can only be suggested by assuming the spectator to take every available position in the temenos.[16]

In the concluding chapter in Martienssen's book is titled "The Greek Achievement," and the first section is: "A General Theory of Related Volumes." The title itself recalls the term relatus which is the aim of this work, and the idea that is gradually delimited in its crossed translations. Relatus as the event-narration, but also a general structure comprising elements that lead to relationships linked to each other and with the past.

Yet an explanation that Martienssen makes in the second section of his concluding chapter is significant. Among the six sanctuaries or acropolis that he selects to study the temene, the three in which the surrounding topography or urban structures do not impose special difficulties are the most valuable for identifying a general model that underpins particular cases: Aegina, Sounion, and Epidaurus. The reasons were similar when it came to selecting the three of Frank Gehry's works chosen for this piece of work,

15. Ibid. Cites Pierre Lavedan, *Histoire de l'urbanisme: Antiquité—moyen* âge (Paris: Laurens, 1926), 142. Translated by Daniel Montero.
16. Ibid., 141.

in other words, the fact that in buildings without topographical conditions or physical precedents, the starting level of abstraction provides us with "laboratory conditions" to identify the tools of the project. Just as zero conditions are created to conduct an experiment in a laboratory, situations that are as neutral as possible are also needed in this architectural examination that we are dealing with here, the projects that have arisen with the starting point of few physical conditions are more usable when it comes to identifying the resources that are repeated in different cases.

According to Martienssen: "Our analyses of specific groups, especially those where outside influence was not so marked as to offer practical difficulties in the course of construction, have provided wide terms of reference within which to seek the criteria of an underlying doctrine."[17]

For Martienssen, the flexibility and repetition of some specific, well-known elements are the main features of the aesthetic model and arrangement system that lie in the origin of the acropolis structure he studies. That systematization, while maintaining basic principles, would offer the capacity to have a broad range of distribution options and the capacity to adapt to the conditions of each place:

> Prime factors that have emerged from our analyses are the extreme flexibility and inherent generalization of element distribution that characterize the sanctuary groups. These factors allow simultaneously an infinitely wide range of plastic experience, and a root similarity of recognizable frameworks in the contributory elements. Thus the kind of experience that is undergone by a spectator is fundamentally the same in each sanctuary, and although wide variations occur in the distances between elements, that experience is the outcome of the application of a central thesis to the material expression of intangible demands.
>
> So far we have examined the temenos as a complete and constructed system which is in process of being "explored" by a moving spectator who is thus assumed to represent a characteristic participant in an actual ceremony taking place within its boundaries. The movement and direction aspects are, in this form of analysis, predominant terms in the space system that arises from the combination of fixed and variable factors. Visual experience is a function (in the mathematical sense) of

17. Ibid., 147.

> this combination and consequently cannot be assessed as an absolute value.[18]

A horizontal surface provides the general structure with physical support.

> The horizontal plane or terrace which "contains" all the elements of the group is the basis on which the system is generated, and which affords formal dimensions and unity.[19]

The *peribolos*, the perimeter wall establishing the limits of the platform, has the task of specifying the complex. The horizontal platform itself can specify the limits in places with a rugged topography, but on flat areas it is established by the peribolos. And it could happen as in the case of Delphi that the agglutinating surface cannot be built upon. In such cases it is the limiting wall of the area that is the unifying element. So the perimeter wall is the first element in the system, which will delimit the precincts in which the relations between the other volumes will subsequently take place. In the projects of Frank Gehry being studied too, it has been seen how the first step in the strategy is the building of those limits. A building that performs the function of a peribolos, or a group of buildings as in the case of the LLS, fixes the precise distinction between the outside and the inside, so that multiple elements can be arranged according to a new general law inside the new precincts.

> The peribolos or enclosing wall contributes vertical definition to the terrace, and separation in the sense of formal demarcation between natural and constructed surroundings. Its chief spatial function is thus the maintenance of material unity in the system. The outcome of terrace and peribolos in combination is an implied volume in which are situated the separate component volumes of propylaea, temple, and statues. Terrace and wall do not provide enclosure, but as we have seen in section I their measuring and defining attributes are such as to formalize space.[20]

In an arrangement understood thus all the elements are participants. In addition to the main buildings, many elements appear

18. Ibid.
19. Ibid, 148.
20. Ibid.

to the traveler along his routes. In the case of the Greeks, the altars, statues or lesser temples. In Gehry's projects the double metal netting around the elevator and the moirée effects it produces, the fountain, the café umbrellas, the boxes that give rise to precincts on the terraces and the geometrical elements located on the roofs, and the trees surrounded by a little piece of lawn on the LLS campus, the isolated and sloping surface of the lawn and the separate parts of the flooring. Everything has an effect on the general structure. They measure and interrupt the route. They limit the scale of the space, and they help to distinguish the new scale of the block from outside.

> Altars and free-standing statues constitute "solid volumes" and these may be regarded as positive interruptions in the continuity of the visually penetrable space that encloses them.[21]

So the basis of these space systems is not dependent on particular elements, it is not conditioned by the location of a single building. The unity of the area can undergo changes, and it is capable of accepting these changes. Changes of a component would transform the routes, and would thus create fresh perspectives. One could think that in the case of the Greek acropolis these groupings were not created out of a single intervention. Elements have been gradually added to them over the years and centuries. Considering that they were the symbol and meeting point of a community, they were living complexes, and over the years statues, altars, commemorative monuments were gradually added to them or replaced. In that respect, they are places that have been accumulating memory, ones that have been gradually formed in the course of time.

In Gehry's case, the Loyola Law School is the most complex of those analysed in this respect. Thirty years have elapsed since the project was started in 1980. The project itself was created as a long-term one, forward as well as backward—since the building that currently houses the Williams M. Rains Library, built in 1964, and the existing car park were incorporated into the building project. The buildings completed in the first phase—Burns, Donovan, Merrifield, 70s, Casassa and the chapel—established the limits of the area together with what had been there before, and established

21. Ibid, 149.

the nature of the campus. Later Founder's Hall was added to it, the campus was extended by means of its "cloister" and the old car park was replaced by a new one. The latest, the Girardi building, went up in 2002. What is more, with the new car park, the proportions of the internal space and some of the interior routes were altered. But the project continues to be the same one, based on the same principles, and the add-ons have enriched it.

> Both elements (temple and propylaea) are thus identified with the space of the temenos, and through the medium of this common factor become related to one another. In terms of these constituents a formal arrangement has been created which approaches closely the perfection of an abstract theorem. It will be seen from this discussion that the essential character of the Greek temenos is not derives basically from size or number so much from the type and special combinations of its structural forms. Scale in relation to human size is necessarily a completing term in the system but the purely quantitative aspect of construction, once this demand has been satisfied, always remains of secondary importance in Greek architecture. Again, when the components subscribe to a system of spatially related yet freely articulated entities within that system, the actual position or number of such elements, though materially influencing the resultant plastic effect, does not modify the intrinsic character that permeates the whole system.[22]

On the last page of his work Martienssen recalls the words of the painters W. W. Jaeger and Amedée Ozenfant. The former to explain the coherence of the theory of the philosophy of the Greeks with their art and poetics. Once again classical oratory is mentioned:

> In the art of oratory, too, their ability to carry out a complex plan and create an organic whole out of many parts.[23]

As a result he highlights a detail that is enlightening in order to understand that link with architecture, that the Greeks' term theoria does not embody rational thought alone, that it has a broader meaning, which also involves perspective. That perspective rep-

22. Ibid., 150.
23. Ibid., 156.

resents all the objects as components within a whole, he sees the idea in all the elements that form the whole.

> The theoria of Greek philosophy was deeply and inherently connected with Greek art and Greek poetry; for it embodied not only rational thought, the element which we think of first, but also (as the name implies) vision, which apprehends every object as a whole, which sees the idea in everything—namely, the visible pattern.[24]

The Kypros.org dictionary gives the following translation of the Greek term *theoria*:

> theoria (θεωρία) = contemplation, speculation, theoretics, theory, view

Ozenfant's quotations confirm the importance of the dynamic perspective in the understanding of the whole in the Greek acropoleis:

> I looked at the harmonious building from every side—far off, close up, closer still. I climbed still. I climbed the side of the hill to see it from another point of view. Everything was changed, yet everything remained beautiful, right. Everything worked together.
>
> But I was not a passive spectator. . . . By my movements, which altered the relationships of the building and of the near and distant objects, I was endowing the view with movement.[25]

In the foreword to Foucault's *The Order of Things*, a further example of the importance of the table as a unifying element of diverse elements can be found, when recalling the following passage in the sixth *Les Chants de Maldoror* of the Comte de Lautréamont, regarded by surrealists as their forerunner.

> I am an expert at judging age from the physiognomic lines of the brow: he is sixteen years and four months of age. He is as handsome as the retractability of the claws in birds of prey; or, again, as the unpredictability of muscular movement in sore of the soft part of the posterior cervical region; or, rather,

24. Ibid.
25. Ibid., 156–57.

> as the perpetual motion rat-trap which is always reset by the trapped animal and which can go on catching rodents indefinitely and works even when hidden under straw; and, above all, as the chance juxtaposition of a sewing machine and an umbrella on a dissecting table![26]

In Foucault's view when umbrellas and sewing machines are unexpectedly found on a table, the table is the space where they meet each other, the possibility of that juxtaposition is ensured by its robustness and presence.[27]

The Significance of the Platform: The Stairs Leading up to the Entrance

As I wanted to explain in the previous point, the specifying of precincts is the first decisive step in the project specification in these three works of Frank Gehry that I am analysing. This specification is made by means of its limits, through a similar procedure to that followed in the case of the Greek peribolos. But in addition to the limits, there is a differentiation of the horizontal plane, too. The surface that supports the internal space is arranged on a more elevated platform. In the main entrance areas of the complex of buildings the presence of the platform is highlighted by means of the creation of a series of steps. Just as in the propylaea, these steps indicate a break, a boundary between the inside and outside.

In these three cases, there is a short staircase between the inside and outside space. At Cabrillo and the LLS one line of the staircase comprising steps is in the pedestrian entrance, three plus a double one in the former, one comprising six in the latter. Each has a ramp on the right-hand side, in the first case limited by two walls and in the second between the walls of the church and Donovan Hall. These staircases resolve a change in level, and initially one could think that they were indispensable. But in view of the starting conditions of the two projects, it is clear that they were also avoidable, and that they have been put there deliberately or intuitively. At Cabrillo the project was created without any precedent, without any urban planning conditions, and there was nothing at all to make a specific height of building obligatory. At the LLS, the height and

26. Lautréamont, *Maldoror*, 216–17.
27. Foucault, *The Order of Things*, xviii–xix.

Top: Entrance to Cabrillo Marine Aquarium

Middle: Entrance to Edgemar

Right: Entrance to Loyola Law School.

Photos by the author.

alignments were established by the street plan, but the size of the plot of land offered a sufficient length to do that staggering naturally inside the plot of land and in the continuation of the sidewalk, even more so since the interior routes are provided with different heights and ups and downs.

However, in the third case, at Edgemar, that staircase does not stand out that much. The entrances toward the inside are on the same plane as the Main Street sidewalks, and these levels are apparent inside, on the stairs that go up to the last two pavilions. Here, the same staircase as at Cabrillo is repeated, almost literally; It has a ramp beside it protected by two walls. In this case the staircase is divided into two parts by means of a ramp, and each of them is aligned with one of the two entrances from the street. If one takes either of these two entrances and follows the line marked by the passage, one comes up against a staircase that will lead one to the main point of the route. The main finishing line of the route ends in the two pavilions, which today house an art gallery, theater, and restaurant. The two entrances function as two streets that lead one to a square.

This different location of various levels is linked to the different natures of the milieus of the projects, and is coherent with them. Cabrillo and the LLS, for different reasons, are located in areas that are foreign. The aquarium is in a spot that comes into conflict with the scale of the beach and car park area with the sea right in front. The Campus is in a tough neighborhood, in an environment dominated by the presence of the scale of the downtown, on the edge of Olympic Boulevard that is one of the main streets crossing the city. What is more, it is a socially conflictive neighborhood in an area with little street activity. Edgemar, on the other hand, is in a comfortable residential district, in a commercial street of Santa Monica that is on a much smaller scale, and fits in naturally with the street opposite it. Its inside opens out toward the street, and for this purpose allows the level of the sidewalk to penetrate it.

Another of Frank Gehry's projects which clearly shows the use made of a flight of steps, is his house in Santa Monica. Here he "plays around" with the shape of the steps. The staircase is divided into two: one arm connects with the sidewalk and the other one rests on the grass. Starting from the bottom the two arms are built of concrete, and in front of the door they are joined together by means of two wooden chests that are randomly positioned and which form the final steps and the access level. This element expresses a radical separation from the street, and as it gradually rises up it expresses the entry into a space of a different nature. This, too, is in some way a propylaeum, because this house is not a temple where a unity already exists, but an open block made up of parts.

Combining Different Scales

One of the features of these systems made up of parts is the capacity to adapt to different scales. In the case of the Greek acropolis, Ozenfant said buildings appeared suitable "from far away, from close-up, from even closer up." The capacity to provide an appropriate response to interpretations that can be made from different distances is also a feature of Gehry's projects, and a consequence of his way of working.

Dividing up the program and breaking the building down into different elements afford him greater freedom to adapt the perception that the spectator will have about the building, as he or she approaches, to a scale of proximity. To the elements that are seen from a distance, as one moves closer, new ones are added, a porch adds a jutting element, the breaking up of a surface, etc.—which will bring about the adapting of the scale that mediates between the building as a whole and the spectator. In the personal formal language he uses, he can add components of a free nature at will without being constrained by a strict, general model.

This capacity is displayed by the buildings of Hans Scharoun, too, among others. He, too, by means of a different formal lexis, dissects a program, and builds it up through elements having a high level of autonomy, "organically" bringing together parts that perform different functions until a whole has been constructed. In the buildings of the Berlin Philharmonic or in the national library there are main volumes that can be seen from a distance, and which establish their place on the scale of a general view of the city. But as the visitor approaches, many other buildings or complements appear, as he or she approaches the entrance; the garden paths require him or her to take one last bend, and when the door is reached a final porch provides the door with final welcoming proportion.

A strategy explained by Frank Gehry explains this resource better. This is what he says in a passage on the effect of art and painting in his work:

> Painting and sculpture influence my work. For instance, when I had the Bellini picture with the Madonna and Child, I originally thought of it as the Madonna-and-Child strategy for architecture. You see a lot of big buildings with a lot of little buildings, little pavilions in front. I attribute that to the Madonna and Child composition.[28]

Madonna and Child, Giovanni Bellini, 1510.
Source: Wikipedia Commons.

The strategy of putting other smaller buildings in front of the main volume, what Gehry calls the "Madonna-and-Child strategy," is what makes the interpretation of different scales possible. In an initial approach, the image of the Madonna appears, and as one moves closer, that of the "Children."

In the same book in which the above paragraph appears, just in the lines above he refers to his forerunners, Wright, Le Corbusier, Aalto is also included in the quotation, and he is perhaps the closest he has come to twentieth-century masters. He writes thus:

28. Friedman, *Gehry Talks*, 44.

> What Aalto did for architecture is what I also like about Hans Scharoun. It's the touch, it's the humanity of it. Wright had that, too. I think Corb has it, but in a different way.[29]

The text that gathers together the two quotations is not linked through a thread of discourse, but a collection of reflections on some specific subjects. Nevertheless, the fact that these two quotations appear one after the other prompts one to think that there is a continuity of thought that links the two together. Aalto, too, and Hans Scharoun in particular, used the "Madonna-and-Child strategy," and this strategy is linked to a kind of humanity, to that welcoming which the building displays toward its users.

I believe that this has a lot to do with the process that Gehry follows in his work. The main tools in his work are the scale models, and the images that will provide the measure of human scale always appear in them. Above all they are the images of small people as well as vehicles and furniture. As the project advances the scale models get bigger and bigger, the level of detail gradually grows, and the scale models are made of the interior spaces of the building on an increasingly bigger scale. In some cases, a complete approximation process is done until gigantic scale models are produced. Tom Hoos described how in the final development phase of the Bilbao project a scale model of the entrance the size of a room was made. The scale of the spaces in that approximation process was so important that in some cases, if a technical installation, for example, required a change to the ceiling afterward, instead of simply lowering it, he would withdraw it and review the shape of that part of the building. [30] As I see it, taking that presence of the human scale in the models is a symptom of that sensibility that Gehry liked in Aalto and Scharoun.

Gehry starts each project with an analysis of the program. He divides the functions that comprise the program into volumes, literally giving each of them a box. These boxes normally have a basic geometry and they are usually wooden or cardboard prisms. With them he does the first arrangement, he forms a three-dimensional diagram. On that level the basic routes of the building, the distribu-

29. Friedman, *Gehry Talks*, 43–44.
30. Tom Hoos is an architect and was Frank Gehry's assistant for many years. In a conversation with the author in San Francisco in January 2010.

tion of functions, the dimensions required by each use are decided. Afterward, and with the sketches he has drawn at the same time, other geometries start to emerge. Initially, they could be crumpled scraps of paper, bits of cloths, pieces of corrugated cardboard, and so on. The function of these elements, even if it might only look like a mere formal search based on intuition, have a much more objective purpose. As the "child" is to the Madonna, they provide the project with the measures of the different scales needed, because there are multiple scales in each project to the insofar as the perspectives are multiple. In that purpose the little people are added without fail to the scale models.

In the following paragraph Gehry expresses this function directly and clearly:

> I'm a strict modernist in the sense of believing in purity, that you shouldn't decorate. And yet buildings need decoration, because they need scaling elements. They need to be human scale, in my opinion. They can't just be faceless things. That's how some modernism failed. When it started getting used by the developers, it became faceless. It became a language that self-destructed. What was missing was human scale.

Here it is possible to detect the existence of a contradiction between first acknowledging oneself to be strictly modern and then going on to express the need for decoration. But what has been analyzed above could banish such a contradiction, because when he refers to decoration he is not talking about ornaments, but about added elements that would provide the building with the right scale.

Use of Materials: The Materiality of Buildings

The use of materials is consistent with the place strategy that is repeated in these three projects of Gehry's. The outside of the elements that establish the limits is done so that they go unnoticed, ordinariness is the main feature in the way they are handled. There are no special volumes or surfaces that stand out and they are of the same kind as those of the surrounding buildings. In addition to delimiting the precincts, they do not reveal anything about what they keep inside. The service doors, emergency elements and installations are located in a natural way, in accordance with pure functionality, leaving the representation for those of the interior.

As one approaches the edges of the arms of the U-shape, around the entrance areas the components that will make up the interior begin to emerge. At Cabrillo, the structure of the stainless steel tubes and galvanized mesh, at Edgemar, the volumes above the cornice that invite one to stop and go inside and different materials at the entrances of the first shops, at the LLS, the copper scales of the chapel and prism tower. The mortar-covered walls, painted white or gray, provide a place for the materials that are raw materials in Frank Gehry's personal catalog from this point onward and all over the inside, galvanized steel tubes, folded plates, scales and nets, plywood, brick surfaces and ceramic.

Loyola Law School, front to Olympic Boulevard. Photo by the author.

Gehry's work becomes rooted in the Los Angeles culture through his choice of materials, among other things. The tradition of the pioneers whereby each person built his own house, the temporary nature of life, attachment to the value of ordinariness–these are all echoes that are recalled by these DIY materials. They are industrial materials, primary transformations that do not conceal the origin of their materiality, the first consequences of the industrialization of building. In that very city they revive the memory of those Case Study Houses that helped to reinvent domestic individuality following World War II: Koenig, Eames, Soriano, Ellwood and others who were the heirs of Neutra and Schindler.

As Rafael Moneo stressed, before he ahieved fame achieved in his later, Gehry had accumulated experience and knowledge of the profession spanning many years, and he knew the reality and techniques of the American construction industry inside-out. The materials and construction systems used in the projects reflected that American pragmatism. The building method is there for all to see, there is no dissimulation. What is more, the visibility of the way of building is one of his most prominent formal features.

Frank Gehry's Early Professional Career: Working with Victor Gruen; The Oxnard Mall

As Frank Gehry himself pointed out, while he was a student the USC School of Architecture,[31] the architects that he found of greatest interest were ones like Richard Neutra, Rudolph Schindler, Raphael Soriano and Harwell Hamilton Harris. But during the last years of his studies when he wanted to start working for a firm of architects, he opted for one that did work on other, bigger scales. He puts the reason for this in the context of his political commitment. Most of the commissions of the architects he liked were for detached houses for the rich, and for someone like himself with a left wing perspective that was not thought to be the most attractive kind of project. That was in the 1950s and he was involved in milieus regarded as left wing. During that era of McCarthyism, his friends were in groups organized to help people in difficulties for being "red."

During those years, Victor Gruen hads one of the few large offices in Los Angeles. The firm undertook projects like subsidized housing, medical institutes and shopping centers. Gehry met several members of the firm in the political meetings, and the fact that Gruen was European was an added reason why Gehry wanted to work with him. After working with Victor Gruen for a time, he went to study at the Harvard School of Design, and following his national service he returned to Los Angeles to work with Gruen.

Victor Gruen (1903–1980) was Austrian, his original name being Viktor David Grünbaum. He studied at the School of Fine Arts in Vienna, and in 1938, like so many other Jews, was forced to escape into exile. He arrived in New York "with eight dollars, an architect's degree and without knowing any English." During the early months he mixed with groups of exiled Jews, and with other refugees from Germany he set up the Refugee Artists Group

31. Boissière, *Gehry, Site, Tigerman*, 13–25.

Ciro facade, Fifth Avenue, New York, 1939. Victor Gruenbaum and Morris Ketchum. Inset: Ciro Plan. Source: Talbot Hamlin, "Some Restaurants and Recent Shops," Pencil Points *20 (August 1939) in M. Jeffrey Hardwick,* Mall Maker: Victor Gruen, Architect of an American Dream

drama company. The first commission he obtained as an architect was a project for a shop in Fifth Avenue in collaboration with Morris Ketchum. In that project, instead of the usual display windows facing the street, the entrance was turned into a gallery which had glass chests on each side.[32] It was a lure to entice buyers. Instead of just piling up the products in an untidy way, they were displayed very carefully in a specially-designed scenography. The model they were proposing was a great success, and after that they received many similar commissions. In 1941, he moved to Los Angeles and set up the Victor Gruen Associates firm.

Being of a left wing persuasion, he was a man who had great faith in planning, and working in the field of retail outlets, and he wanted to propose a new city model for American citizens around these retail outlets. The project that consolidated his success was the Southdale mall in the town of Edina in Minnesota. Frank Gehry also worked on this project. Gruen's proposals set out to revolutionize the model of shopping centers existing until that moment.

32. Hardwick, *Mall Maker*, 24–26.

He turned the building housing the shops totally inward, inside a box that appeared completely closed to the exterior. The shops, which until that moment used to be arranged on a single floor, were put on two floors, and could be visited comfortably by means of an escalator and a lift. In the middle of the complex he created a space similar to a square, which had fountains, a huge cage full of birds of different colours, trees, a pond, balconies with plants hanging from them, and a cafe.

> It is our belief that there is much need for actual shopping centers—market places that are also centers of community and cultural activity. We are convinced that the real shopping center will be the most profitable type of chain store location yet developed, for the simple reason that it will include features to induce people to drive considerable distances to enjoy its advantages. - Victor Gruen, 1948.

But Gruen's model was even more ambitious. For him the shopping center was simply the center of a complete new city development; he also envisioned apartment buildings around it, homes, a health center, a park and a lake. In Gehry's words, Gruen was concerned about the city, and his plan was to create new hubs in the residential neighborhoods of American cities, "new suburban town centers," that would be arranged around public spaces for walking around on foot.[33] But the success of Gruen's projects took a very different direction. He dreamed of a new space that would encompass the city life of Vienna's Ringstrasse, but during the last years that he spent in America he was able to see how shopping centers turned into isolated boxes surrounded by car parks the size of an ocean.[34]

Working in Gruen's office gave Frank Gehry a practical perspective on building, and he has always maintained this awareness of the importance of clients and budgets. He also learned how to manage the organization of working teams and the dynamics of a large office. There he worked on large-scale building projects, which he describes as fairly ordinary buildings: office blocks, shopping centers and large-scale town planning projects. In these works he

---

33. Conversation between Frank Gehry and Thomas Pritzker, Aspen, CO, March 7, 2009.
34. Gladwell, Malcolm. "The Terrazzo Jungle" article, *The New Yorker*, March 15, 2004.

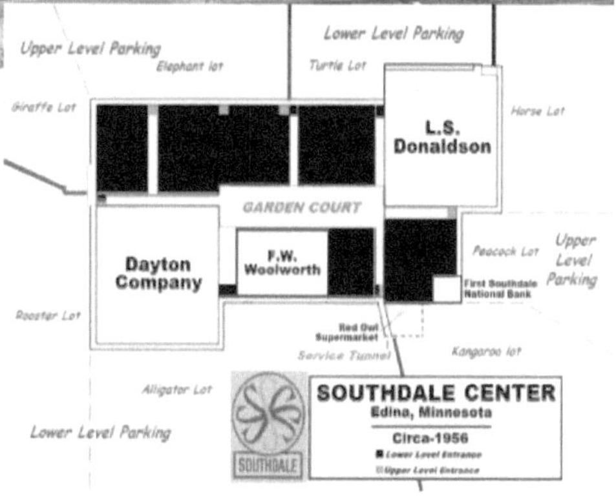

Above: Aerial view of Southdale Center, Edina, Minnesota. Source: Minnesota Historical Society

Right: Southdale Plan, circa 1950s

Bottom: Southdale Garden Court

Upper Level Parking
Elephant lot
Lower Level Parking
Turtle Lot
Giraffe Lot
Horse Lot
L.S. Donaldson
GARDEN COURT
Dayton Company
F.W. Woolworth
Peacock Lot
Upper Level Parking
First Southdale National Bank
Rooster Lot
Red Owl Supermarket
Service Tunnel
Kangaroo lot
Alligator Lot
Lower Level Parking
SOUTHDALE
SOUTHDALE CENTER
Edina, Minnesota
Circa-1956
Lower Level Entrance
Upper Level Entrance

Centerpoint Mall, Oxnard, California. Photos by the author.

developed his skills with standard and commercial building systems. This knowledge had a significant impact subsequently on his individual projects.

According to Michael Sorkin, there are few hints pointing to the nature of the genius of Gehry's professional work in the early years of his career. The only evidence, in his opinion, is the experience he accumulated over many years while working on shopping malls.

> Search as one does for hints of things to come, there is little to recommend itself as the harbinger of genius. Acceptable corporate design, always decent, but never especially innovative, was the order of the day. The only hint of the future lay in Gehry's long experience with the shopping mall. The paradigmatic mall is binucleared like the family, mama and papa anchors holding up opposite ends of an enclosed family room around which cluster the lesser shops, the children of the arrangement. This mall party informs many of Gehry's works, from his first big independent project—the actual mall in Santa Monica—through the Loyola Campus, and culminating, after a long voyage, with Bilbao, creating spaces deployed around a central "atrium" that organizes functions around it.[35]

One of the last projects he did with Gruen is the Centerpoint Mall Shopping Center in the town of Oxnard. Even though this project was basically like many other malls, it is possible to pick out many elements there which were to appear in Frank Gehry's works. In the center of the mall there is a covered street on one floor which receives natural light from the ceiling. Around this main block there are two main volumes, which are the locations for the "anchor" retail outlets. Although the block forms a whole, the parts comprising it are distinguished from each other, each one having a distinct material and formal nuance. The upper part of the façade along the entire length comprises the central alley and creates a continuous portico beneath. This shadow line breaks up the volume and the pavilion appears as a narrow, horizontal brown ribbon. There are hardly any openings outward, except for a small shop or access up to the offices. It has entrances on its two edges, supplied with plants, which cross from one side to the other and provide an entrance from each side of the car parks.

---

35. Sorkin, *Some Assembly Required*, 99.

By contrast, the volumes on the edges are of a different type. Although they are attached to the first one, they are autonomous as far as their composition is concerned and appear as a solid volume. At their entrances we can find volume compositions that recall Californian Art Deco of the 1930s or certain postmodern elements of the 1970s: cylindrical pillars with a large diameter and porticos completed with elemental geometrical figures, of the same type as those which will also be found later on in Gehry's work, in the halls at Loyola, for example. These distinctive elements make up a distinct composition in each case, those of one building having nothing to do with those of the other.

In the place where the main volume has a dark, rough stucco, the ones on the edges have a smooth surface painted white or green. Other materials appear in the elements marking out the entrances. In one, a white portico comprising a symmetrical composition supported by square pillars, higher in the middle and sloping on the two sides. The pillars have a rough surface and green pedestals, and the beams that rise above the openings between the pillars are covered with green tiles and the cornice is red. In the pavilion on the opposite side the volume is the main one which is staggered to achieve greater height, and is expressed by means of horizontal, curved cornices in the entrance. The cornice is supported by cylindrical pillars and both the cornice and the pillars are covered with plates of greyish aluminium.

Although the three main buildings appear aligned and continuous, the points where they meet are highlighted, because of the entrances of the volumes and the changes in materials. That way, without breaking the canon of the mall, each part is presented in a distinct way.

In the main gallery at Oxnard certain features that can be found in Gehry's early work can also be identified. The structure is wooden and even though the exterior and interior blocking off points cover it almost completely, in the skylight that runs all the way along the gallery and in the upper windows that illuminate the entrances from two sides, the structure appears bare. The wooden planks of the structure that is built using the platform-frame system appear bare on these points. Instead of interrupting the structure and adding a piece of carpentry, the exterior surface is simply cut off when it reaches the edge of the gap, and wooden rafters continue, they

Interior, main gallery, Centerpoint Mall, Oxnard, California.
Photos by the author.

Cabrillo Marine Aquarium, exposition area. Photos by the author.

cross the gap and fulfil the purpose of woodwork that supports the glass, similar to that of a curtain wall. On the edges of the interior surface that has been cut off, no trims have been added. That way, a single, simple built detail is achieved and no complicated parts are used. The logic of the building system is put above any formal preconceptions, so that its own built details can be accomplished.

Another trace of that simplicity of the building system is the way of positioning the false ceilings and installations. The ceilings are achieved through clean, hanging planes, in the form of autonomous planes without reaching the walls. Here, too, when the two elements are articulated through an empty gap, no special joints between the different materials are used, and the detail is accomplished in a clear, economical way. From the inside of the building the water and power installations remain visible. Thanks to that they are arranged according to the logic of their functional needs, and their presence is accepted as another component of the block.

These building criteria have always been maintained in Gehry's works and they are to a certain extent the consequence of pragmatism. Above any formal preconceptions, building resolutions are chosen on the basis of their functionality and simplicity, in favor of building logic. This attitude is also evident in the three projects analyzed.

The structure inside the exhibition center at Cabrillo is totally visible. The installations can also be seen, and in this case this decision turns out to be very important. In the aquarium complex the installations are needed to supply the tanks where the sea creatures are kept; they require constant maintenance and have to be flexible so they can be adapted to changes in the exhibition. Leaving them visible greatly facilitates this work. One is struck in that respect by the solution of the floor which has been provided with paving stones placed directly onto the sand, which allows the installations that go along underneath to be registered. At Cabrillo, moreover, the tendency to show the structure and installations is consistent with the philosophy of the organization, with the desire that the visitors should get to know the activity of a laboratory rather than an exhibition.

In the lecture hall, too, the structure is visible and to achieve the acoustic adaptation the noise absorbers are simply hung there, as are the ventilation pipes and lighting installations. The clearest solution is given to the combination of all the components needed for adapting it to its functions, they are not concealed and are left visible.

The old pavilions preserved at Edgemar have a ceiling with vaulting geometry, built by means of wooden trusses. That structure was repaired and preserved, and inside its partitions, skylights and new installations were added. The old structures and the new elements combine with each other without any problem. The crossings are made without any transition or concealment. In this case, this naturalness is totally logical, because Gehry's formal world has its origin in the same building tradition in which these pavilions were built.

At the Loyola Law School these features can be found on a more refined, developed level. An example of this is the way that all the installations in the building of the Fritz B. Burns Academic Center run along the corridors. The most normal thing in such cases is to conceal the installations by means of a false ceiling and put the lighting there. Yet here no second ceiling is created. The structure remains visible, and the folded metal sheets that make up the lower part of the floor are visible. The air conditioning, water supply, sprinkler system in the event of a fire, the electrical installations and all the other elements remain visible. Everything is painted white like the walls of the corridors, and in that unity of colour, and properly arranged, they form a tidy whole. The lighting system is accomplished with the maximum modesty. Fluorescent tubes are suspended from the ceiling, protected by screens that project the light upward. These solutions are even more striking in the Students Lounge, because it is a room for events and because the installation network produced there is also more complex. Here the acoustic fittings are achieved through a free plane that hangs from the ceiling under the installations.

This method of building, which juxtaposes the building's components without any transition, freely and austerely, is evident anywhere throughout these projects. Another example is how the metal façade of the new car park at the LLS is linked to the concrete framework. But the most prominent and most beautiful example appearing in the buildings that are being analyzed is the LLS's Merrifield Hall. It is the largest classroom on the campus and is a stepped platform like most of the rest. Its structure is made of

Above and right: Edgemar, inside views of reused pavilions. Photos by the author.

Above: Student lounge, Loyola Law School. Left: Burns Building corridor, Loyola Law School. Photos by the author.

Above: Merrifield Hall, interior
Preceding page, top: Merrifield Hall, entrance
Preceding page, middle, bottom: Merrifield Hall, details.
Bottom: Merrifield Hall, interior.
Photos by the author.

wooden trusses, and is a volume which has a gabled roof and square ground plan. On the exterior, ordinary blue doors form the entrance, and two red doors form the emergency exits at the back. All the added components attached to it to fulfil and express its function are free-standing elements that meet through juxtaposition.

Outside, a ramp that goes up from the axis of the building to the door indicates the importance of the hall in the hierarchy of the campus. A staircase reaches the height difference that the classroom has in the interior, and forms a stylobate. Two prisms with square ground plans that do not touch the building form a classical composition on each side of the door. These pillars are covered with copper in an attempt to highlight the importance of the Hall through the quality of the material for it.

By contrast, inside Merrifield there are no representative elements. The structure of the cover is made of wooden trusses and is visible; hanging from it are some wooden frames and the lower surface of these frames are counterveneer planks. As in a concert hall the purpose of these hanging planes is to project the speakers' voices properly in the hall. The lighting equipment is incorporated into the planks. The ceiling panels closest to the stage are enclosed in a transparent polycarbonate instead of in wood. They allow the light from the skylight in the ceiling to pass, and at the same time the frames supporting the planks remain visible. The side and back walls of the hall also have counterveneer planks, with holes for acoustic purposes and turned toward the stage. The floor is carpeted and the seats are comfortable but are ordinary classroom ones.

The planks on the ceiling do not touch each other and between them the structure and all the installations are visible to the eye. The back of the lighting equipment can also be seen. Each element performs its function by being joined to those next to them through juxtaposition. The result is a volume of complex geometry and materiality, but as in the case of the public space of the whole campus, it is made up of simple components that have a simple geometry.

After the years spent with Gruen, Gehry explains the evolution in his perspective with respect to building.[36] Gruen's design partner was another Viennese, a perfectionist in his work, who designed complex building details. Gehry learnt the nuts and bolts of the

36. Frank Gehry and Thomas Pritzker, interview, Aspen, March 7, 2009.

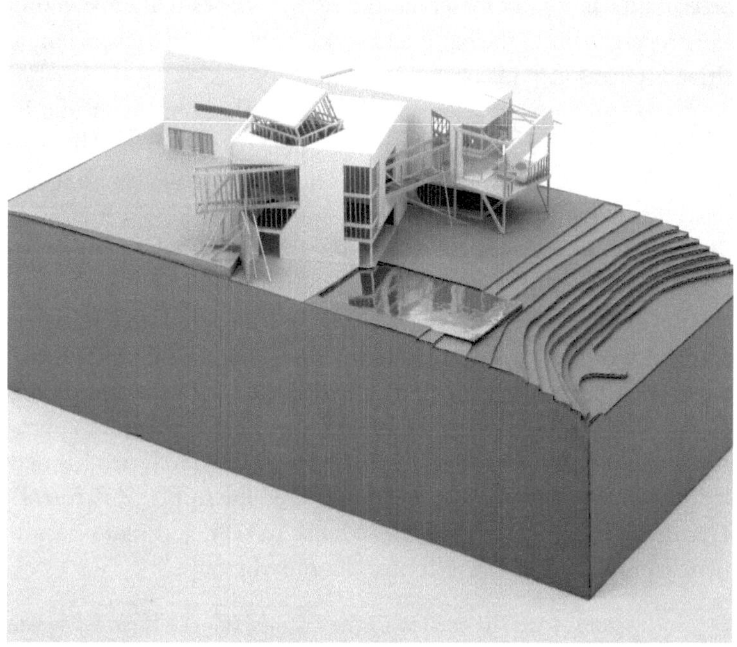

Familian House Project, Santa Monica, California, 1977–1978, Frank Gehry. Source: Courtesy of the Museum of Modern Art, New York

profession in Gruen's office, to organize large working teams to do large-scale projects, and that was of use to him to start out on his own.

But that way of building was expensive, "no one had a large enough budget to do that," and that drove him to desperation. Moreover, that way did not coincide completely with his personal way of thinking and concerns. On the one hand, he had been deeply influenced by classical Japanese architecture during the years he was studying. Many of the teachers at the school were enthusiastic about it, and that timber architecture could be done in California. On the other hand, he found the wooden structures that were being built in California more attractive during the construction process than when they were finished. He found the wooden structures more attractive than the appearance of the finished buildings.

He was a very close follower of the art that was being done in those years and was greatly interested in artists like Jasper Johns and Robert Rauschenberg. He was fascinated by the works these artists did using junk materials and by the shapes that appeared in the process to build the big tract houses, and he tried to incorporate these interests into his professional work.

He began to work with corrugated metal sheets, metal meshes, with counterveneer planks, bare wooden structures. All these materials were cheap, and common in the American building industry. But they were hardly given any prominence in buildings. They were components on a secondary level. Gehry put them in the foreground.

The early projects he did on his own in the 1960s still followed the course of the years he had spent with Gruen, but the bare structures and cheap materials gradually emerged in his work, particularly from 1976 onward. Small-scale projects were more appropriate for research and that is how he gradually developed his new language: Ron Davis's house (1972), Gemini G.E.L. (1976–99), Gunther House (1978), Wagner House (1978), and more prominently in the 1978 Santa Monica "Familian House."

> I guess I was interested in the unfinished—or the quality you find in paintings by Jackson Pollock, for instance, of de Kooning, or Cézanne, that look like the paint was just applied. The very finished, polished, every-detail-perfect kind of architecture seemed to me not to have that quality. I wanted to try that out in a building. The obvious way to go about it was the unfinished wood studs. We all like buildings in construction better than we do finished—I think most of us agree on that. The structure is always so much more poetic than the finished thing —Frank Gehry[37]

He literally embarked on the process to undress the structure in his own house. As he says, few people were prepared to build houses like that, and the opportunity for research presented itself when he himself was the client. He bought a wooden, two-storey detached house in Santa Monica. The plot did have planning permission for an extension, albeit a small one. The project kept the existing house, and in the narrow strip around it he added a single-storey volume.

To join the new and the old together he removed the planks covering the walls of the original house and left the wooden skel-

37. Arnell, Peter and Bickford, Ted, "Frank Gehry: Buildings and Projects." Rizzoli International Publications, New York, 1985. 6.

eton bare. The result looked like an unfinished building, like those he liked so much in the intermediate phases in the building process. He made the new parts of the façade using those cheap materials, counterveneer planks, corrugated metal and metal mesh. This house turned into a kind of manifesto of the concerns that mattered to him.

In recent years, the materials in Gehry's projects have changed considerably, particularly since the success of the Bilbao project. The shapes became more complicated, complex curved surfaces appeared, and he started to use more expensive material—stainless steel, copper, titanium, stone. Budgets, too, have changed a lot and computers provided an opportunity to study more difficult building systems. But his building system retains that concern of the early years. The acceptance of building elements and the audacity in leaving things visible (in Bilbao, the metal structure of the entrance, the inside stairs and the tower beside the bridge; the steel framework supporting the surface of the Disney Concert Hall) and the tendency to resolve the building details in an austere way (the curtain walls of Bilbao, for example) can still be picked out in his projects.

Over the last fifteen or twenty years Frank Gehry has effortlessly received praise for inventing the shapes he created. But leaving formal criteria on one side, as much merit is due to these inventions as to having created a professional structure which has enabled them to be built.

Through the capacity provided by computers, today the main concern of his office is to develop a new system for organizing the building process. As Gehry says, with the new systems for organizing the work made possible by technology, architects can achieve greater control over the building process. Just as architects dominated the work in the past, the new programs can put the architect's office and the contractor in direct communication with each other without any intermediary. Gehry Partners today is immersed in the use of these tools for communication.

> The most important thing is that the computer gives us a tool we can use to communicate with the contractors. . . . The new computer and management system allows us to unite all the players—the contractor, the engineer, the architect—with one modeling system. It's the master builder principle. I think it makes the architect more the parent and the contractor

> more the child—the reverse of the twentieth-century system. It's interesting because you wouldn't think that would happen with something as technical as the computer but, in fact, it has. And you wouldn't think an office like ours would lead it. Nobody else does it yet. But they will.[38]

Bricoleur

The DIY reference in Frank Gehry's work is a double one. As Alejandro Zaera recalls in the analysis of his work, the paradigm of "bricoleur" used by Claude Lévi-Strauss in his work *The Savage Mind* could fit it.[39] According to him, unlike an engineer's all-embracing, planned project, the bricoleur engages in one-off solutions, using the resources that he or she has to hand and in accordance with the freedom that is afforded to him or her. The tools used by a bricoleur on a specific job have not been specially created for this or that project and for this or that moment, but are the ones that are to hand or which in the course of time have been accumulated at different opportunities. The composition of the whole is not linked to the project, but with all the possibilities he or she has to renew and enrich the stock or to reinvent using the previous building or demolition.

A result of this, the continuity of the themes through the projects, the identification of a line of formal pieces of research. Accepting the imbalance of comparisons, as in the space idea of the Greeks put forward by Martienssen, it gathers together the components of a familiar catalogue into a set of precincts.

Incorporating Preexisting Elements into the Project

The capacity to integrate preexisting built elements into a new "event" block is one of the features of these relatus. A strategy seeking diversity could not simply abandon them. As regards the projects in this study, they are the main pieces of evidence of the consistency of this way of doing things.

At Edgemar and at the Loyola Law School, previously built elements on the plot of the project were already there. In another

38. Friedman, *Gehry Talks*, 51–52.
39. Lévi-Strauss, *The Savage Mind*, 16–20.

project these buildings could be understood as an obstacle to the project. Instead, in the case of Edgemar and that of the LLS, they have been understood as the seed of an urban block and around them a kind of "community" has been built. The result of the project is enriched by the including of these previous elements.

In the case of Edgemar, the very name is also an additional component of what those buildings had been, and regarding the toponymic name as fixed, links the new project with the past of the location, like preserving the old Art Deco façade of the shop. Keeping the latter part was a condition set by the administration, but the capacity to take it over without falling into mimeticism reveals the capacity for goodness of the building strategy that is being analyzed.

At Loyola the William M. Rains library was the building that was there first. It was the only building of the LLS from 1964 up until the 1980s when the new buildings were created. When Gehry got down to the project, he visualized the whole campus starting with the existing building. The Rains building has ended up as part of the square of the alignment of buildings that form the perimeter.

The strategy of the project used easily accepts foreign elements, because its structure is not based on a stylistic unity, but on the relations created among the elements that form the whole. Although in his projects the material features of each building become very powerful and stand out, the consistency of the whole does not lie in those specific features, but in the formation of the whole that provides them with unity. As a result, the old industrial buildings fit in naturally as at Edgemar, or a building like the Rains of the 1960s.

Relationship with the Surroundings: External Surfaces

In these projects, unlike in many of this other projects, the surface facing the exterior is totally neutral, it does not stand out more than necessary against the surroundings. In Bilbao or at the Disney auditorium, or previously at his home, even if the complexity of the shapes looks outward, in these other ones what faces outward is very plain indeed, and variety is reserved for the inside. There are some elements that stand out from the outside, the objects on top of the cover of Edgemar and the net and fish images at Cabrillo, but in the two cases they are interior objects that stick out to herald what is enclosed inside. They are not the main components, but add-ons. Like the elements that invite one to go inside, they inform about the events that take place inside.

In the case of Loyola, what stands out particularly is the wish to distinguish between the external and internal surfaces. In all the new buildings that have gone up inside the perimeter, except the car park, the façades facing the streets are finished in a grey base coat, but all the other façades of the same volume are painted in bright colours. And in the case of the car park, even though the façades are initially similar—those of a standard car park—the internal façade has a "false" steel surface attached to it. It repeats the composition of windows of the long, yellow side of the Burns building as if it were disguised in garments on the scale of the others. The chapel too, despite being at the entrance, has its back to the access; its wooden structure is concealed from the outside and faces inside.

Interior Organization

In addition to the materials, the geometry of volumes is also transformed as one moves from the exterior to the interior of the projects. One moves from orthogonal prisms to volumes of unknown shapes, objects with a symbolic function start to participate in the game, and the homogeneity of the whole is lost as it gives way to the juxtaposition of different parts. In that breaking up of the whole, fresh affinities are created. They are the components of a new location.

The geometry catalog, the language he uses, gives him freedom to approach the users in another way, too. In a much freer way than that of a specific language. The dividing up of the building's elements affords him freedom from the general order or arrangement, and below the general arrangement provides him with the opportunity to work on different scales at the same time. His work is developed in the comings and goings between the sketches and scale models, and the major decisions are taken in the working models. What is striking is the fact that in these models human figures always appear in the form of little dolls, in addition to cars and trucks, and they all constantly provide a reference and measure of the scale. The break in the unity of the project allows the author to take the right decision on each part, to accumulate different interpretations one on top of the other on the same spot, thus creating a plural reality. So that each entrance, each space, can have the character he wants to give it, provided by the materials and dimensions, without being subordinate to a general composition. Thanks to the pieces of geometry he has accumulated in his stock, Gehry's buildings are able to respond appropriately to the different scales, from the moment they are situated in the distance in the town/city or countryside to the point where the visitor opens the door and goes inside.

The defining moment in Frank Gehry's career was the time when he completed his house, Santa Monica Place. From that moment onward his deepest concerns and his professional career began to merge. As Michael Sorkin says, that change did not take place through the inventing of a new language, or through a sudden leap made to new forms, "but with the breath of new life injected into old forms." Although Gehry's forms may be "wild," his strategies with respect to the location are calm and precise.

> The city is the ultimate architectural ensemble, and Gehry's urbanism is, at the end of the day, fundamentally respectful of the accumulated conventions of the historic. While the forms may be wild, the strategies of situation are both calm and precise.[40]

The mastery in solving the leap between the expansion area of Bilbao by means of the museum entrance and the foyer and the riverbank is proof of this. The whole is a new narration, it has the structure of a new relatus, different parts are sewn together through a new line of argument, in a new relationship without losing their autonomy. The interpretation of the whole is the result of particular entities, creating a new open narrative instead of building a spatial, hierarchical arrangement.

Marcel Proust's Gaze

The explanations that Frank Gehry gives for the references underpinning his work are few and far between. "I'm a craftsman" was the way in which he described himself once. Seeing the way he works, the fact that he likes this description makes sense. His projects are

---

40. Sorkin, *Some Assembly Required*, 100–1.

born directly out of his scale models, out of the contact he has with the materiality of the project. His concerns, too, are in the sphere of the direct relationship between what is planned and the actual building. He has based a large portion of the development of his work on that relationship, for example the 3D systems for architecture that are being developed on the Catia platform through the Gehry Technologies Enterprise together with IBM.

That being so, the references he has had published on the work or theory of other architects are few and far between. That is why it is worth bearing in mind that when being questioned about his preferred reading material he answers that he always has Marcel Proust close to hand. When he presented the LVMH project he was moved by the fact that he was going to work near the Bois de Boulogne where Proust had walked on so many occasions.

> You know, whenever I go to a museum I fall in love with something—Boticelli's Primavera, for example- but each time I see differently from last time. Today I would look at the fabrics. And I would see it architecturally, whereas I never saw it that way before. When I drive I'm listening to Proust now. I read Proust thirty years ago. I slogged through it; I wasn't ready. Now I just go nuts. I play it over and over. When he describes the town, when he describes the room, when he describes the hills, the sky.[41]

Furthermore, in a public interview he gave at Yale in 2006 with Paul Golberger, while they were talking about the reading and music that had exerted an influence on his work, and when asked whether he had been influenced by Joyce or Chomsky, he mentioned Proust. What appeals to him about Proust is the author's capacity to capture "fleeting glimpses of thoughts" by means of words. He said that in the creative process of architecture, too, the forms, in the midst of speculation, are somehow "dreamed up," and that if they are not grasped at that moment, they escape.

Proust's gaze unendingly penetrates what he sees; whether it is the buildings, the landscape, human feelings, behavior, he examines and describes them again and again, wanting to exhaust all possible perspectives and approaches. He examines all aspects of the reality of the most commonplace things, returning to one and the same

41. Friedman, *Gehry Talks*, 44.

subject along different paths. Over and over again he examines the detail of any attitude, the feelings that a certain place evokes in him, his own reflections, too, so that he can capture the smallest aspects. He moves under the surface of things, seeking out what is hidden beneath. As Gehry says, he follows the trace left behind in his memory by the fleeting glimpse.

In the following passage, Proust describes the emotion he felt when he saw the perspectives of the church towers that appeared in the landscape on the journey he made one afternoon in the doctor's cart with his parents when he was a child, while they traveled to and from the neighboring village:

> At a bend in the road I experienced, suddenly, that special pleasure which was unlike any other, on catchin sight of the twin steeples of Martinville, bathed in setting sun and constantly changing their position with the movement of the carriage and the windings of the road, and then of a third steeple, that if Vieuxvicq, which, although separated from them by a hill and a valley, and rising from rather higher ground in the distance, appeared nonetheless to be standing by their side.
>
> In noticing and registered the shape of their spires, their shifting lines, the sunny warmth of their surfaces, I felt that I was not penetrating to the core of my impression, that something more lay behind that mobility, that luminosity, something which they seemed at once to conceal and to contain.
>
> The steeples appeared so distant, and we seemed to be getting so little nearer them, that I was astonished when, a few minutes later, we drew up outside the church of Martinville. I did not know the reason for the pleasure I had felt on seeing them from the horizon, and the business of trying to discover that reason seemed to me irksome; I wanted to store away in my mind those shifting, sunlit planes and, for the time being, to think of them no more. And it is probable that, had I done so, those two steeples would have gone to join the medley of trees and roofs and scents and sounds I had noticed and set apart because of the obscure pleasure they had given me which I had never fully explored. I got down from the box to talk to my parents while we waited for the doctor to reappear. Then it was time to set off again, and I resumed my seat, turning my head to look back once more at the steeples, of which, a little later, I caught a farewell glimpse at a turn in the road. The coachman, who seemed little inclined for conversation, having barely acknowledged my remarks, I was obliged

> in default of the other company, to fall back on my own, and to attempt to recapture the vision of my steeples. And presently their outlines and their sunlit surfaces, as though they had been a sort of rind, peeled away; something of what they had concealed from me becamse apparent; a thought came into my mind which had not existed for me a moment earlier, framing itself in words in my head; and the pleasure which the first sight of them had given me was so greatly enhanced that, overpowered by a sort of intoxication, I could no longer think of anything else. At that moment, as were already some way from Martinville, turned my head I caught sight of them again, quite black this time, for the sun had meanwhile set. From time to time a turn in the road would sweep them out of sight; then they came into view for the last time, and finally I could see them no more.[42]

In the volumes *In Search of Lost Time*, the excerpt that probably displays the greatest connection with the capacity of architecture to accumulate memories is in the seventh volume *Time Regained.* It is where the main character, immersed in his reflections, gets ready to go inside the Guermantes house and treads on a paving stone that is set slightly deeper than the rest. At that precise moment, he loses his balance and this has the effect of bringing his memories flooding back. Driven by the rush of joy he experiences, he decides to gather together all these memories and set about writing them down. The loop in Proust's work is thus completed. [43]

The experience that the Israeli writer Liel Leivobitz had when he tried to translate Proust's text into Hebrew is interesting regarding the gaze with which Proust saw reality. A fan of Proust ever since he was young, he set about translating À la *recherche du temps perdu.* But he found it impossible to translate Proust's French into the Hebrew of Israel of the end of the twentieth century. Resigned, he had to drop his plan. But he continued to be captivated by Proust's way of writing. Several years later at the age of twenty-four when he left the army and decided to go abroad, he realized while he was in Paris what it was Proust himself that attracted him: what he refers to as the "Jewish perspective" of the world, the attitude of seeking complexity that is below what is apparently simple. He explains it thus:

42. Proust, *Swann's Way*, 253–55.
43. Proust, *Time Regained*, 230–31.

As the Talmudists knew, only when we produce pages of commentary for every word in the scriptures can we truly get at their meaning; as Proust realized, only when we write at great length and intricacy can we truly get a closer look at the machinations of life.

This, I believe, is very much our Jewish heritage, as well as our key literary mission. Let the Hemingways punch out their short, declarative sentences. For us, a nation of priests, literature—and life—is about the beauty of complication, the grace of difficulty, the savagery of truth.[44]

Alvar Aalto's Influence

This resource, the use of the U arrangement, has also been used by Alvar Aalto in some of his projects. An element that forms a U-shape at the town hall of Saynatsalo has its back to a mountain slope and on the opposite side that faces the town another building is positioned to close it off. Here, too, two openings remain on both sides of the building that acts as a plug. In each one steps rise up to resolve the gradient between the street and the inside courtyard. They are distinguished from each other by means of the pavement and the geometry. The steps leading to the main entrance are made of paving stones, while the other is of an irregular geometry with grass covered steps supported by wooden planks.

Inside there is another invention here, too, an artificial hill is created, as if the Town Hall had been moved to the top of a hill in a town that is largely flat. As in the case of Cabrillo, that illusion does not go the whole way, because the ground floor of the building is accessible throughout its perimeter on the lower level, but an interruption that is much bigger than the true distance is created between the inside of the courtyard and the surroundings. As Marc Treib asserts "for those sites that lacked potent natural features Aalto constructed his own architectural landscapes."[45]

The source of this invented topography could be found in the influence Italian landscapes had on Alvar Aalto. The way many Italian villages are located in the landscape on top of a hill or small mountain is a theme that is repeated in Aalto's travel sketches, and there is no doubt that therein lies the origin of the invented land-

44. Leibovitz, "Lost in Translation," n.p.
45. Treib, "Aalto's Nature," 55.

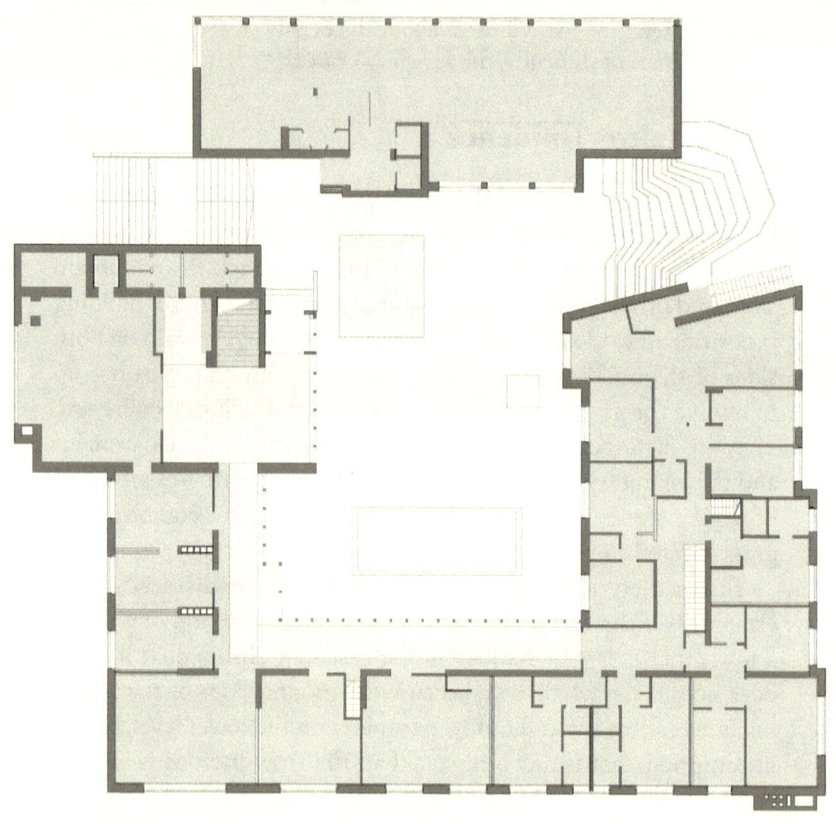

Alvar Aalto, Saynatsalo main floor. Redrawn by the author.

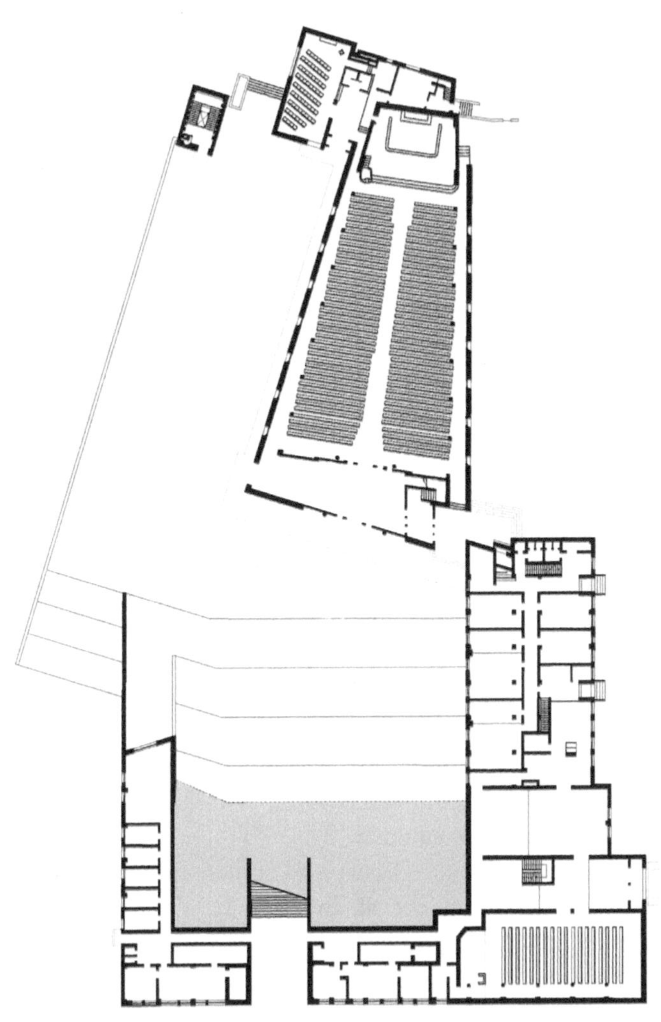

Alvar Aalto, Seinajoki church and parish center. Redrawn by the author.

scape that is created in this project at Saynatsalo.

> In my mind there is always a journey to Italy: it may be a past journey that still lives on in my memory; it may be a journey I am making or perhaps a journey I am planning. Be this as it may, such is a condition sine qua non for my architectural work.[46]

Aalto used similar tools in the project for the center of Seinäjoki, in a more developed way corresponding to the much greater size and complexity of the project. The elements forming his project are arranged around a central axis, and around this axis paths of varying importance are incorporated here and there into this axis. The town is bigger than Saynatsalo and its flatness stands out more. A topographical tabula rasa was the area chosen for locating a complex that had to be the main public buildings and new city center. Here, too, the project has transformed the topography, and above the main horizontality two new hills have been created at the entrances of the two main institutions, the town hall and the church. The result is a more complicated landscape, which symbolically locates the buildings of the institutions on top of new hills, and which recalls the Italian reference he loves so much.

The arrangement of the church complex deserves particular attention. It comprises the church itself, the tower and the parish hall and even though the main organizer is the axis that starts from the temple, the diversity of entrances causes many different routes to cross. That way a plural complex is formed through the juxtaposition of many elements that have distinctive features, made up of sequences that can link different routes. The different entrances put many surrounding spaces in a relationship with the lawns that form the center of the church complex.

This time the use of the U-shape takes place on different levels. The main one is the temple itself. The lower buildings of the parish hall form a U-shape and the temple itself is what is placed in the middle of the opening. Here too, it has been turned thus giving priority to the access on one side. The second entrance remains hidden when seen from certain points, but as one approaches it is a passage that creates an important link up toward the last building that re-

46. Aalto, in *Casabella* magazine, 1954. Source: Treib, "Aalto's Nature," 62.

mains outside the main arrangement. On another level, the passage between the church and the tower does a doubling act, even though in this case the second gap is no more than a narrow area between the wall and the tower.

As in previous cases, the space retained in the middle by the church complex, the inside of the U-shape, is kept separate from its surroundings and creates the illusion of a new landscape. It is a smooth, grass-covered slope, which takes us up to an observatory in the center of a plateau and which dominates the complex, and during specific celebrations can fulfil the function of an extension to the temple. But more than anything it is a transformation of the topography, a fresh reality.

> Like the buildings themselves, the complex is a collage of varying parts. An opening through the parish services wing admits the visitor to the court before the church, but the view is skewed and skirts the façade. Throughout the complex, the visitor's glance is diverted; the structures demand no perpendicular confrontation in the classical sense. The space is, in fact, more a dynamic path than a restrained plaza, more emphatically suggesting movement than stasis.[47]

So, here too, as in Gehry's projects, the arrangement of the buildings and the organization of their parts continually break up and recompose the view of the visitor, and so that he or she is forced to see partial views of the complex. The perception of space adapts to the structure of a time sequence of spatial and formal events, creating a kind of spatial relatus.

This U-shape technique that Alvar Aalto uses was highlighted by Manuel Iñiguez, too, in his work *Time and Place in the Work of K. F. Schinkel and A. Aalto*. Having gone back in search of similarities, he found a precursor of that use in Schinkel's Glienicke project.[48] A similar resource referred to in this work emerged, a delimiting U-shaped building which specifies an interior space within it, and on the open side a fence element, another built volume, which closes the courtyard and leaves two accesses. Here, too, by making one of the arms of the U-shape shorter and turning the closing element by a few degrees, a hierarchy is produced between the two gaps

47. Treib, "Aalto's Nature," 61.

48. Iñiguez, *Time and Place in the Work of K.F. Schinkel and A. Aalto.*

which interrupts the static nature of the interior space. The two entrances that give onto the courtyard have distinct features as in the previous cases, one with paving stones and pergolas, and the other open and covered with grass.

It bears many similarities with the work of Alvar Aalto[49] and Gehry himself is said to have once acknowledged that affinity. Another feature that is repeated in the works of both of them is the material and formal ordinariness of the secondary level elements that intervene in the complex. They form the backdrop for the volumes that are given prominence. As in Gehry's work, the simplicity of the volumes that form the ancillary services around the church also stand out in Seinäjoki. And also the simplicity of the volumes which, at the opposite end of the main axis, culminate the route beyond the town hall and auditorium.

On a trip there with students from the Faculty of Architecture, I heard someone make the following comment while we were at the latter: "And is this Alto's? It looks like an apartment block in Malaga." Beyond the sensibility of the person who said this, the comment indicates that the different approaches among the different parts are evident. This aspect is also highlighted by Demetri Porphyrios who is quoted in various pieces of work about Aalto's work. When remarking on the resources used by Aalto in the Rovaniemi project that bears great similarities, he points out:

> The monuments are not the Town Hall, the theater, the library, or the church in toto but rather the assembly room, the auditorium, the book stacks and the basilica-campanile themselves. The pronounced design of these monument-fragments and their gift for impromptu composition distinguishes them from the nondescript fabric which sustains them and to which they are attached.

In other words, here too among the elements that form the whole, can be found on the one hand, built volumes that form a neutral backdrop, and on the other hand, the "monuments" that appear on the stage formed by them.

Another feature linked to the above is arranging the volumes of the buildings according to a breaking up of the program. When

---

49. See Porphyrios, *Sources of Modern Eclecticism*, for a discussion of Aalto's work.

Alvar Aalto, Saynatsalo Town Hall. Source: Kimmo Virtanen.

Gehry explains how he works, he describes how when he embarks on a new project, the first thing he does is to break up the program. After that he fleshes out each of these parts in a part of the scale model, and with these parts he analyzes how the program works and how the building fits together. The system of working with these scale models is very likely the most significant element of Gehry's work, and also what distinguishes him most. In the opinion of Rafael Moneo, these scale models are more than the representation of an architecture in Gehry's case, they are architecture.

The relationship that a project will have with its surroundings during its development is identified by Gehry as a chess game, but that metaphor can also be applied to the composing work he does with the parts of the building. In a sequence in Sydney Pollack's film *Sketches of Frank Gehry*, he is seen working with one of these scale models with his collaborators; it is a continuous sequence of change-wait-examine-change, until the solution that will satisfy him is achieved. This is reminiscent of a sentence in a conversation with Jorge Oteiza when referring to the work to write his poetry: "I take a sheet of paper, I write one, two or three words . . . and I wait."

This composition of the various pieces appears in Alvar Aalto's work, too. Seeing the whole made up by the service buildings behind the hospital of Paimio reminds one of the accumulation of objects in Gehry's projects. The chimney and the volumes enclosing it could have had a place in the Californian's catalogue. In Aalto's work the Viipuri library is one of the works that best represents the development made on that way toward projection. From the first version that won him an award to what he produced in the end, he progressed from a compact classical model to the placing of each element of the program into its corresponding, specified volume, and the shape of the building emerges as the sum of these parts. This change is not to be found solely in the arrangement of the main volumes. In the interior elements too, the different components start to become more autonomous, like the ceiling of the assembly room made up of waves, or the library shelves, or the ceiling of the reading room full of light holes. This breaking up of the elements of the program became a permanent feature in Aalto's work, and in Gehry's case it made possible that diversity of complexes referred to above.

To describe Aalto's work, Demetri Porphyrios uses the concept heterotopia to refer to "the order that regarded Western rationalism as disordered," as opposed to the homotopia of rationalism. He takes the term in its literal sense to mean "the situation of the things that are located in different ways and which makes it impossible to define a common locus between them.".He cites two categories in the sensibility of heterotopia: discriminatio and convenientia. The main feature of the second one is the juxtaposition between different elements, parataxis. It is worth drawing attention to the term "adjacency" used again and again in an interview given by Frank Gehry's former assistant Tom Hoos when describing Gehry's working method; once the components of a project had been established, their "adjacency," was worked on in the various scale models.

In Anglo Saxon countries there is a custom of setting aside certain places in parks specifically for children; they are known as Adventure Playgrounds and children are allowed to build their own huts with the materials, bits of wood, tree trunks, planks and other raw materials left there for them,[50] so that they can build heterotopias according to Foucault's terms. In these three projects, too, a kind of adventure playground can be marked out. Thus, the hanging fish appear at Cabrillo, the hanging metal mesh, the ramp and the objects above the ceiling at Edgemar, or the little temples at the Loyola Law School.

The Importance of the Context in Frank Gehry's Projects

Gehry himself has said that published photos of his buildings mostly do not include the context and therefore fail to show where they have originated, and that this has led to misunderstandings on occasions.

> Europeans who have seen pictures of the buildings do not see what is around them, and do not see that it is a very contextual building in a very traditional sense. I bought in the same things you did, except mine are weird, because it is a chaotic environment made from some kind of new government called democracy. . . . I do not think the context is a bad thing to deal with, in fact it is almost a deal with the social structure,

50. Marot, *Suburbanismo y el arte de la memoria.*

> with what has gone on before.[51]

As an example, he cited the American center in Paris, the disappointment of some critics for whom the project did not live up to their expectations, in other words, it was far removed from the way he tackle d his other projects. Gehry justifies the difference that could exist between this project and his other work by attributing the special nature of the context, and that the context is important in his work and, as a result, that building is largely a reflection of the feelings he has about Paris. The built context of Paris exerted a direct influence on the choice of materials and geometry.

He explains how, when starting to work in a new location, he analyses the changes caused by the new elements in the location. He describes this strategy as if it were a game of chess:

> It's like a chess game with you the next move on the table, and by making this next move you make the whole better than it was, and if it is appropriate, you steal the center stage. If it is the case of something like a concert hall, I feel that is appropriate.[52]

The analysis of that *chess game* played with the context could clarify, below the surface of formal similarities, the process followed in each project.

When reading what has been written about Gehry's work, what is striking is how the analysis of the relationship he has with the plastic artists has prevailed over the research into sources and links that he might have in the field of architecture.

This approach is understandable, when one has an idea of the special nature of his formal catalogue. If one ignores the relationship his projects have had starting with their gestation with the context, and if one fails to examine how the program, which of necessity has to be drawn up because they are works of architecture, one could even go as far as taking into consideration the materiality of the finished buildings alone. Once one has put oneself in that perspective, the content is restricted to the special nature of the formal catalogue. To that must also be added that his way of working is consistent with not wanting to establish any theoretical

51. Jencks, "Individual Imagination and Cultural Criticism," 17. Comment by Frank Gehry.
52. Ibid.

teaching, and that he uses very pragmatic forms of arguments in the explanations of his projects. It could appear on occasion that these "down-to-earth" explanations of his have been interpreted as a gesture of modesty in academic circles, and the fact that they could conceal deeper rationales has been ignored.

By making approaches from these positions, it is normal to seek the most important references in the plastic artists and to regard his work as being without references in the field of architecture. They are not incorrect searches, but they leave a whole field unexamined.

However, in some analyses made from the field of architecture, that attitude of his with respect to the location and specifically with the city has not gone unnoticed. Significant in this respect is the title of the lecture he delivered in 1994 at the Royal Academy, "Since I'm so Democratic I Accept Conformists" and that of the book published on the basis of it, *Individual Imagination and Cultural Conservatism*. In the foreword of this book, Charles Jencks quotes directly from T. S. Elliot's essay "Tradition and Individual Talent."[53]

But the forum that was also published as part of the Jencks book also demonstrated the different directions taken when interpreting Frank Gehry's work. While Will Aslop, Peter Cook and Paul Finch were examining it from the perspective of architecture done outside the urban context on the peripheries of the city, the point made by Adam Caruso was significant. He pointed out that it was a mistake to link the work of Will Aslop and Gehry together, and then cited the relationship between his attitude with respect to the context and the works of conceptual sculptors and artists:

> What I found so inspiring about Gehry's architecture is that it is engaging in a profound way with where it is coming from, both within a political and physical context. I would like to point out from that work the use that Gehry makes of certain Post-Modernist conceptual sculptors or artists who have worked with those concepts. They inform the way Gehry's buildings respond and come out of their context.[54]

He later went on to refer to Richard Serra as being among those artists who work with the context, specifically his work "Tilted Arc." And later on, the words addressed to Charles Jencks on the attitude

53. Jencks, "Frank O. Gehry," 6.
54. Jencks, "Individual Imagination and Cultural Criticism," 31. Comment by Adam Caruso.

toward the city context right at the time when the discussion sparked off by the Prince of Wales was still alive in Great Britain:

> Regarding those traditional city centres which you have described, Charles, I think it is a case of how we imagine it, and the regard in which we hold it varies from age to age, along with our historicizing and our fictionalization. So I would argue that the forces which you are trying to relegate to the suburbs are actually active in the centre of the city. Frank interests me because he recognizes that.[55]

In other words, it is identified as an architectural strategy fed by 1960s art and taken to the network of the city center to interact with the context.

When referring to Gehry's work during a Walter Gropius lecture in 1990, Rafael Moneo admitted he was uncomfortable with the word "contextualism," because it could evoke the mimetic response to the context. Instead of that, he chose the word "property."

> Property, to be appropriated, means to respond, replicate, react, but without the prior prescription that signifies knowing what has to be done.[56]

That property implies no formal prejudgments, but involves an appropriate response to the context.

Different Strategies Used by Frank Gehry in Other Projects

When the starting conditions were different, the project strategies used by Frank Gehry were also different, despite the formal catalogue of built elements he used being similar. Among the most prominent cases I should like to refer to are: the Bilbao Guggenheim Museum and the Disney Concert Hall in Los Angeles, because they constitute two milestones in his career, and because the study of the similarities and differences in strategy could clarify the themes above.

We have seen that in the locations in which the references are

---

55. Ibid., 32.

56. Moneo, Rafael. "Reflexiones a propósito de dos salas de conciertos: Gehry Versus Venturi." Walter Gropius Lecture, Graduate School of Design, Harvard University, April 1990.

more neutral, the first thing Gehry does is to carry out a delimitation, to create a field of play through it, and how, within that place that he has created, he builds a new relatus through elements of his personal creation. But in some other projects, the "places" are already there, and due to the relationship they have with the context they have strong features. They are internal city plots and suggest a more specific interpretation because of their position in the city network. The projects have their starting points in the interpretations of the place.

Guggenheim Bilbao Museum

The starting point for the Bilbao project is totally different from the previous ones. Here the place itself had many prominent determining features. It already had around it the structured, stable urban network of the expansion area. There was also an industry memory that offered different levels of interpretation. With the side of the Artxanda mountain right opposite, the limits of the plot of land were established between the Ibaizabal river and the platform of the city expansion area, so the field of play did not need to be delimited, it was already established. And there was also what I consider to be the main component, there was a building with which to make a start: the Salve bridge.

When three architects were asked to submit their bids to build the museum, the first location proposed was the Alhóndiga by the architect Bastida. Apparently, that location was felt to be too restricted and unsuitable, and a selection was made among other possible choices. From the various versions of what happened, it is not clear who chose the definitive location. According to some versions, it was Thomas Krens who was the head of the Solomon R. Guggenheim foundation at the time. According to what is suggested by other versions, it was Frank Gehry himself. Whatever actually happened, and bearing his works in mind, one could be led to think that Gehry was likely to have been fascinated by the structure of the Salve bridge with its asymmetrical structure offering an entrance to the expansion area along the route from the side of the Artxanda mountain. Seeing its concrete columns on the right hand edge, the lift towers and stairs, and the columns and cables of the metal structure supporting the bridge must have filled him with a passion to connect with it.

La Salve Bridge from inside the Bilbao Guggenheim. Photo by the author.

The Salve Bridge has a curious structure. From the right hand side it crosses the river down a slope and descends to the expansion area. Its structure is composed of parts that distinguish its function and its material. On the right hand side there are thick, tall concrete pillars, which produce a principal rafter and the platform of the bridge placed on top. On each side two lifts connect the path along the riverbank with the top of the bridge, and concrete steps spiralling up highlight its height. On the left hand side, two metal columns rise up on top of another concrete portico, they stand on the bridge and support the road hanging from four cables attached to triangular heads. It is not a canonical bridge that composes a formal unity, it is made of different parts, each with a shape and function in accordance with the function it fulfils. The bridge's lack of unity comes close to Gehry's architecture. Its metal part has as much connection with the concrete part as it has with the museum's structure.

As borne out by the scale models, this piece of engineering is by no means foreign to Gehry's building, and the museum turned it into one of its components right from the start. What is more, if one were to propose removing a part of the building, the bridge would most likely be the most untouchable part. If it were removed, it would leave the building orphaned. To fit in with the museum, there was no need to add the questionable red garment that Daniel Buren added to it in 2007.

The location had already been formed by the bridge, the building was located under its protection, embracing it from underneath. Upriver, on the other side of the bridge, through the structure rising up on the Uribitarte docks, an arm rises up and clutches the bridge, just as if it were holding on to it so as not to be carried downriver by the water.

The connection with the bridge has connotations of even greater significance. It is unlike the connection it could have with another kind of building, the ubiety of the bridge is more powerful. In his essay "Building Dwelling Thinking," Martin Heidegger wrote that a bridge is not built in a place, but rather it creates the place once it has been built. It joins two banks together, with each other and with the river. And they are linked by what goes into the distance by crossing the bridge, and also to the distant places that the road is heading toward.

> The bridge swings over the stream "with ease and power." It does no just connect the banks that are already there. The banks emerge as banks only as the bridge crosses the stream. The bridge designedly causes them to lie across from each other. One side is set off from the other by the bridge. Nor do the banks stretch along the stream as indifferent border strips of the dry land. With the banks, the bridge brings to the stream the one and the other expanse of landscape lying behind them. It brings stream and bank and land into each other's neighborhood. The bridge *gathers* the earth as landscape around the stream. Thus it guides and attends the stream through the meadows. . . .
>
> The bridge lets the stream run its course and at the same time grants their way to mortals so that they may come and go from shore to shore. . . . Always and ever differently the bridge escorts the lingering and hastening ways of men to and fro, so that they may get to other banks and in the end, as mortals, to the other side. . . .
>
> Thus the bridge does not first come to a location to stand in it; rather, a location comes into existence only by virtue of the bridge.[57]

57. Heidegger, "Building Dwelling Thinking," 330–32.

We can reflect on what the bridge contributes to the museum building: it connects it to the two sides, to the river, to the roads, and through them, to a broader tract of land. A building made of shapes that twist because they sought movement "starts" by means of the bridge. The movement metaphor takes shape when the structure of the building merges with the comings and goings of the people that cross it along their route. And at the same time, it builds the metaphor of an institution that wants to spread its contents from a specific location. Perhaps through the two ponds it is the very metaphor that seeks images of a ship that is on the water's surface in those estuary docks of the Ibaizabal River.

The second major feature of the project, regarding its relationship with the location, is the masterstroke: which ocurrs when the break between the expansion area and the river is stitched together. The museum connects the considerable difference existing between the two levels through its entrance, reminiscent of what was created by Francisco Saenz de Oiza at the entrance of the Basilica of Aranzazu (1950). One has to descend a ramp toward the entrance as if it were a jetty.

The Bilbao Guggenheim's expansion area-entrance-door-balcony-river sequence is one of the most successful solutions that can be found for a complex urban passage, which was difficult to solve, as borne out by the subsequent attempt made by Arata Isozaki five hundred meters upriver. In the last step of that sequence, owing to the difficulties in bringing the river itself close to the building due to the water quality and the tides, the scenography resource used to conceal the edge between a pond and the river by means of a curved bridge also deserves a mention.

Numerous elements forming the museum building make complete sense in that relationship with the surroundings. The long Fish Gallery under the bridge penetrates as far as the other side; the tower structure at the end of the gallery embraces the bridge and unifies the perspective of the two from the Uribitarte docks; the ponds and bridge on the edge link it with the river; the entrance square provides a finish for the expansion area platform and is linked by a ramp; the blue office buildings, together with the other buildings in the Alameda Mazarredo, form an arrival portico for the road that reaches the expansion area from the bridge; Jeff Koons' Puppy also becomes a part of the building, forming a "Ma-

Above and below: La Salve Bridge and Bilbao Guggenheim. Source: El Correo.

This and facing page: views of the Disney Concert Hall (DCH), Los Angeles

This page, top: view of downtown from rooftop; upper left and above: DCH from 2nd and Hope intersection. Lower left and below: DCH from above and below Grand Avenue.

Facing page: top: rooftop garden. upper left: garden; middle upper left: Lillian Disney Memorial Fountain; middle lower left: stairway to garden; lower left: rooftop public garden. Upper right: rooftop public garden; middle right: Keck Children's Amphitheater; lower right: rooftop public garden

Photos by the author.

Preceding page and above: sequence of eight photos from a walk around the DCH auditorium. Below: sequence of four photos from a walk around DCH between auditorium and Founders Hall. Photos by the author.

donna and Child" composition; and the long flight of steps and the wall that finish it off on the Abandoibarra side form the limit between the building and the lack of precision further down.

With respect to the latter it could be said that the wall built on the Abandoibarra side is the only thing that establishes a new limit. It is the hardest face of the building, because that is where the hardest side of the context is located. It is basically an empty public space without any scale, which has over the years been gradually filled with all manner of objects. The wall has provided the museum building with a plinth. It provides the separate titanium volumes with a unity to face the scale of that distant perspective. It would be difficult to give the building a finish similar to the one it has in Uribitarte on the Abandoibarra side. There, the building gradually breaks up into its branches, until it slowly disappears into the docks and pond. But on the Abandoibarra side it not only has to address the change of gradient, but also the change in scale, and perhaps that is why it resembles a fortress. Putting a line of stone protection in front of the titanium, the museum delimits the plot of land, in the way that ramparts do. This limit protects it from the elements that will eventually be built at the foot of it later on. This tactic will be seen once again, more prominently, in the Disney Concert Hall project.

Disney Concert Hall, Los Angeles

According to a widely held opinion, the Los Angeles downtown or city center is said to be an example of very poor urban planning in the United States. As it is a city with a low density spread over a broad piece of land, the commercial and leisure life contained within its center lacks the usual bustle. No crowds of pedestrians are seen in the streets, little use is made of public transport, and for years it has been regarded as a dangerous place.

In that atmosphere the quality of public space is not good. Although there are some parks, there is no coherent public space network on a par with that of San Francisco or of New York, in particular. The fact that the car is the main form of transport also influences the use of the empty spaces, and many of the plots of land in the city center are used for parking.

Its relationship with its surroundings is uneasy, too. Multiple-lane freeways form a ring around the city, and the closest suburbs on the other side of the freeways, the Pico suburb where the Loyola Law School is located, for example, are mostly poor quality areas. So its continuity with the other suburbs of the city is limited.

The land downtown is not flat, it is built around a hill, and the Disney Concert Hall is built at the top of it. To understand the relationship this building has with its context, you have to bear in mind that no one goes there on foot. It is a hall that can hold 2,300 people with a car park for 2,500 cars beneath it. The building that houses the auditorium is surrounded by a stone wall. That wall has the height of a single floor on the 1st Avenue side, and it gains height as 2nd Street and Hope Street go down, until it reaches a height of four stories at the junction between the two streets. The wall forming the perimeter is continuous and on the side facing 2nd Street, has an extra story added to it.

The only side on which this perimeter is broken is the one facing Grand Avenue. This avenue runs horizontally in this part and links several public buildings together: the Museum of Contemporary Art (Arata Isozaki, 1986), the Cathedral of Our Lady of the Angel (Rafael Moneo, 2002) and together with Disney, the Performing Arts Center of Los Angeles County comprising the Dorothy Chandler Pavilion, the Ahmanson Theater and the Mark Taper Forum. Together they form a neighborhood for cultural events, which Michael Sorkin describes as an acropolis, and Disney opens out to the axis of this complex which is Grand Avenue. The cafes and main hall are located there.

Nevertheless, in the direction connected with the city, Grand Avenue is a bridge. There is another avenue of the same width underneath it, which serves the basements of the skyscrapers and the MOCA. The bridge of the avenue ends at 2nd Street, right where the DCH rises up. So, from that side, it can be interpreted as a bridge that links the city center with the fortress.

At the DCH, a public space is arranged on top of the walls forming the perimeter; it is a walled garden. There are two sets of steps leading up there, at the corners of Grand Avenue—2nd Street and 1st Street—Hope. The flights of steps are hard, they cut any link with the street, and so the garden is cut off from the street, giving one the sensation that one is entering a protected, hidden area.

Even though it is possible to enter directly from the sidewalk level at Grand Avenue, the main entrance is located at the corner

Facing page: Walt Disney Concert Hall, garden level.
Courtesy of Gehry Partners, LLC

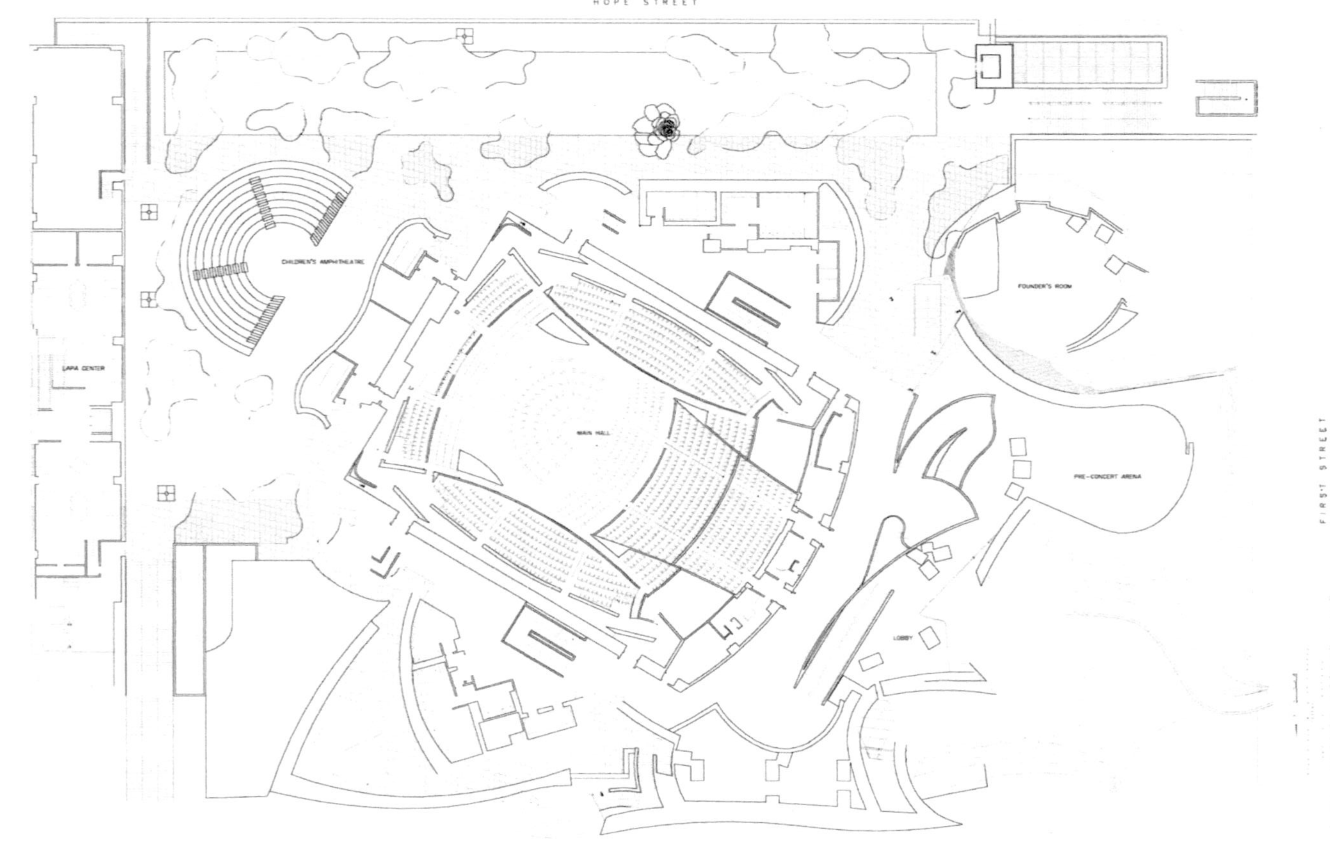
HOPE STREET
CHILDREN'S AMPHITHEATRE
FOUNDER'S ROOM
SECOND STREET
MAIN HALL
PRE-CONCERT ARENA
FIRST STREET
LOBBY
GRAND AVENUE

where Grand Avenue and 1st Street meet, next to the Dorothy Chandler, and it is raised from the street level at the height of the perimeter wall. To get to the entrance one has go up a flight of steps between the two volumes that conceal the entrance.

The scale of the garden has nothing to do with its surroundings, with the huge car park and the broad sidewalk. It is intimist and despite being public it has a private air due to its scale. It is not like the public spaces analyzed in the first projects. In them the center of the complex was empty, and the buildings were arranged around them. Here, on the other hand, the volume of the auditorium is in the middle, and the surroundings are empty. It is so big that the volume of the concert hall reduces the garden space, and in some places even turns it into a narrow passage.

The sensations when entering the Disney garden are similar to those felt when walking around a medieval European fortress. It was designed by Melinda Taylor and Associates. As pointed out already, to get there you have to go up a long flight of steps and you get a clear feeling that you are going up to a platform. Once there, and as has been seen in the other projects, one comes across a complex made up of differentiated objects and places. Going up the steps on the northern side and entering the garden on the left is a little building where the Founder's Room is located. The shapes of its volume almost coincide with that of the concert hall, but its surface steel is brighter and that is what distinguishes it from the concert hall. It is the child in a Madonna-and-Child composition.

As one walks through the garden the next place to stop can be picked out between the branches of the trees. The trees planted are low ones located among shrubs and flowers, and little paths for one person or small groups to walk along pass through them. In a space where there are no trees there is a flower-shaped fountain, the Lillian Disney Memorial Fountain. It has leaves made of concrete and steel and covered with pieces of Royal Delft china, as a tribute to the person after whom it is named.

As one progresses further, one comes across a steel shell, standing upright, and beneath it a small open amphitheater. It is the W. M. Keck Foundation Children's Auditorium. Open concerts are held for children there as part of an education program.

One can either cross through the auditorium or approach it from either side. It conceals the views seen so far from anyone walking through the garden. From the outside one can either continue through the garden or go behind the acoustic shell of the stage. If one takes the second option, one has to cross a narrow passage which reminds one of the rock art sculptures that Richard Serra has at the Bilbao Guggenheim.

Once one has passed the amphitheater one arrives at a small square. That is also an open space left among the trees. A circle of paving stones expresses the unique nature, the simplicity of the space. But what looks like a circle is not a circle but a spiral. Instead of expressing a static destination, it marks out a stopping place linked to the route. One reaches that square from the stairs ascending from the south side, and from there the offices have their entrance.

The volume of the offices is what adds an extra floor at the front of 2nd Street, and from that side it is what provides the perimeter with increased height. It hides the views seen up until that moment from whoever has been walking around inside the garden. Until one gets there, the garden follows the cornice of the perimeter, and offers unparalleled views of the city. But the perspective is hampered by the office volume when one arrives at this south-western façade, on the spot where one confronts the center skyline face to face.

When one leaves the square one has reached the end of the garden, but the route continues. It turns into a narrow path, which can only be used by a maximum of two people side by side. It is a winding path because it follows the surface of the auditorium. After walking along the path a little way, a flight of steps appears, and as one approaches one realizes that it is an observatory. One goes up the steps and there one finds oneself, as if one has ascended the highest edge of a fortress, on the triangle of the bows of a ship face to face, with the most spectacular view of the downtown skyscrapers. The view which earlier had been hidden by the offices as one comes through the garden, dramatically appears all of a sudden. It is a triangular observatory, pointed and only a few people can be there at the same time. Like the whole route, it is one to be explored alone.

After that, the path continues as if along a narrow passage. It goes all the way around the auditorium, like the battlements that protect the cornice of a castle. It meets another flight of steps that goes up on the Grand Avenue side, the third to the top of the wall, and as it approaches the corner of 1st Street it goes on rising, through steps that bend in a zig-zag shape. Along this way what the path shows are dramatic perspectives of the main foyer and the metal skeleton that supports a rustproof steel surface. This is an intimist view that is the opposite of the garden which was facing outward completely. Finally, when the route comes to an end, after going round the auditorium, it returns to the side of the Founder's Room by means of a flight of steps.

Because of its bypass nature, this path that embraces the auditorium is linear. But as we have seen in other projects, there are many different entrances, and the possibilities are multiplied in the expansion areas. Some of the elements of the inside circulation of the auditorium also fulfil the function of providing emergency exits.

As in fortresses, above all what from outside is a wall and inside it, a network of spaces on a small scale can be found above the Disney Concert Hall. It is a place that offers protection and rest in the midst of surroundings that are hostile for the walker.

The building also prepares a dramatic welcome for those arriving by car. From the main hall, continuing like a single space, descends a staircase that penetrates under its base. Almost without break this volume coincides with the platform and the steps that lead to the entrance into the auditorium. The visitors reach this open space in the center of the building from all the floors of the car park, and between walls painted red they slowly and mechanically ascend from the bowels of the building.

To support this fortress interpretation of the Disney Concert Hall, Gehry wanted its surface built entirely of stone, as well as the part comprising the auditorium. If he had done so, the whole of it would have been built in one single material. But he had great difficulty having curved shapes produced in stone, and even though technically it could be done, it apparently would have dramatically put up the budget. They tried to adapt it to forms that could be made with a smaller quantity of different pieces of stone, but in the end for economic reasons, they had to give up and the surfaces surrounding the auditorium had to be made of steel and were thus distinguished from the stone base.

The stone flower that could not be built ended up as a smaller one by way of a gesture at the Lillian Disney memorial fountain in the garden.

Conclusion

Disney's Castles

The castle is the most identifiable image in the world of Disney. Despite there being different versions, "Cinderella Castle" in Orlando and Tokyo, "Sleeping Beauty Castle" in Anaheim and Hong Kong, "Le Chateau de la Belle au Bois Dormant" in Paris there are all variations of the same model, versions of the castle that Walt Disney depicted in the tale of Sleeping Beauty.

To represent that castle he took inspiration from the castle of Neuschwanstein in Bavaria, which was built on the orders of King Ludwig II of Bavaria and completed in 1886. Significant too is that this castle, which inspired what is the symbol of the best-known theme park, was created out of the imagination of a painter, Christian Jank, who made the scenographies for Wagner's operas. The project for it was later executed by the architect Eduard Riedel.

So Disney's castle, which we can take as a symbol of twentieth-century fantasy architecture, the castle that was to become the company's symbol and image for the presentations of his films was created from a fortress that was the result of a romantic interpretation of the Middle Ages.

That being the case, saying that the Disney Concert Hall on Bunker Hill was built to resemble a castle could be regarded as a joke. It might be a step too far to think that the interpretation of its relatus that I have made here was consciously created by Gehry.

But the comparison of the two projects, Disney's Sleeping Beauty castle and Gehry's Disney Concert Hall, puts the two methods of analysis used in this piece of work face to face with each other.

The first one has built a narrative structure through fantasy.

More than a leisure place, and beyond that, it has built a relatus that has made a place for itself in the collective memory, and which embodies the place Disney occupies in modern popular culture. Besides that, Gehry also offers the narrative structure of a castle, as a public building, too. But this time the tools used are not the fantasies of a romantic opera scenography, nor a historical fiction that could be closer to credibility. He has built a project that has the spatial narrative structure of a castle, but he has done it from the formal catalogue created from the exploration of the building techniques of his time and context. On top of Bunker Hill the Disney Concert Hall is a castle.

Cinderella Castle, Walt Disney Resort, Florida. Source: ShajiA via Wikipedia Commons.

Disney Concert Hall from Downtown. Photo by the author.

I once wrote a story . . . about a man who was injured and taken to a hospital. When they began surgery on him, they discovered that he was an android, not a human, but that he did not know it. They had to break the news to him. Almost at once, Mr. Garson Poole discovered that his reality consisted of punched tape passing from reel to reel in his chest. Fascinated, he began to fill in some of the punched holes and add new ones. Immediately, his world changed. A flock of ducks flew through the room when he punched one new hole in the tape. Finally he cut the tape entirely, whereupon the world disappeared. However, it also disappeared for the other characters in the story . . . which makes no sense, if you think about it. Unless the other characters were figments of his punched-tape fantasy. Which I guess is what they were.

— Philip Dick, "How to Build a Universe That Doesn't Fall Apart Two Days Later," 261.

Bibliography

Abalos, Iñaki. *Atlas pintoresco.* Volume 1. *El observatorio.* Barcelona: Gustavo Gili, 2005.

Alexander, Christopher. *El lenguaje de patrones.* Barcelona: Gustavo Gili, 1980.

Arean, Antonio, José Ángel Vaquero, and Juan Casariego, "Madrid 1 Tiempo 2." *Arquitectura COAM,* no. 293 (1992): 1–15.

Ballard, J.G. *Cocaine Nights.* London: Harper Perennial, 2006.

Barnes, Julian. *England, England.* Vintage Books: London, 2008.

Baudrillard, Jean. *America.* Translated into English by Chris Turner. London: Verso, 1988.

Bergson, Henri. *Matter and Memory.* Translated by Nancy Margaret Paul and W. Scott Palmer. London: George Allen, 1913. Translation of *Matière et mémoire* [1896].

Blundell Jones, Peter. "Discovering Hugo Haring." *Architectural Review* (2001).

Boissière, Olivier. *Gehry, Site, Tigerman: Trois portraits de l'artiste en architecte.* Paris: Editions du Moniteur, 1981.

Borges, Jorge Luis. "The Analytical Language of John Wilkins." Translated by Lilia Graciela Vázquez. At www.alamut.com/subj/artiface/language/johnWilkins.html, last modified July 17, 1999. Another translation by Ruth L. C. Simms can be found in *Other Inquisitions.*

———. "The Creation of P. H. Gosse." In *Other Inquisitions, 1937–1952.* Translated by Ruth L. C. Simms, 22–25. Austin: University of Texas Press, 1975.

Bechtler, Cristina. *Frank O. Gehry / Kurt W. Foster.* Osfildern-Ruit: Cantz, 1999.

Brainard, Joe. *I Remember*. New York: Granary Books, 2001.

Brosa, Victor. *Alvar Aalto*. Barcelona: Ediciones del Serbal, 1998.

Carrère, Emanuel. *I Am Alive and You Are Dead: A Journey into the Mind of Philip K. Dick*. Translated by Timothy Bent. New York: Metropolitan Books, 2004.

Caruso, Adam. "The Emotional City." In *The Feeling of Things*. Barcelona: Polígrafa, 2008.

———. "Traditions." In *As built: Caruso St John Architects*. Gazteiz: A+T, 2005.

Celant, Germano. *Frank Gehry: Buildings and Projects*. New York: Rizzoli, 1985.

Choay, Françoise. *The Invention of the Historic Monument*. Translated by Lauren M. O'Connell. Cambridge: Cambridge University Press, 2001.

———. *Pour une antropologie de l'espace*. Paris: Editions du Seuil, 2006.

———. *L'urbanisme: Utopies et réalités; Une anthologie*. Paris: Éditions du Seuil, 1965.

Collins, George, andChristiane Crasemann Collins, Christiane. *Camillo Sitte: The Birth of Modern City Planning; with a Translation of the 1889 Austrian Edition of His* City Planning According to Artistic Principles. Mineola, NY: Dover Publications Inc., 2006.

Colomina, Beatriz. "Una conversación con Frank Gehry: El proceso del proyecto; Gehry de la A a la Z." *El Croquis*, 45 + 74/75, 2006.

Davis, Mike. *City of Quartz: Excavating the Future in Los Angeles*. New York: Vintage Books, 1992.

———. "Fortress Los Angeles." In *Variations on a Theme Park: The New American City and the End of Public Space*, edited by Michael Sorkin, 154–80. New York: Hill & Wang/Noonday Press, 1992.

Dick, Philip K. *The Collected Stories of Philip K. Dick*. Volume 1. *Beyond Lies the Wub*. Los Angeles: Underwood/Miller, 1987.

———. "How to Build a Universe that Doesn't Fall Apart Two Days Later (1978, 1985)." In *The Shifting Realities of Philip K. Dick: Selected Literary and Philosophical Writings*. Edited by Lawrence Sutin, 259–280. New York: Vintage, 1995.

Eco, Umberto. *The Mysterious Flame of Queen Loana*. New York:

Houghton Mifflin, 2005.

Egaña, Andoni. *Hogeita bina*. San Sebastian-Donostia: Hariadna editoriala, 2004.

Eliot, T.S. *The Sacred Wood: Essays on Poetry and Criticism*, "Tradition and Individual Talent." London: Methune, 1920.

Evensen Lazo, Caroline. *Frank Gehry*. Minneapolis: Twenty-First Century Books, 2006.

Filler, Martin. *Gehry's Urbanism: Critique of Loyola Law School and Spiller House*. Skyline, October 1982.

Foucault, Michel. *The Order of Things: An Archeology of the Human Sciences*. New York: Pantheon, 1970.

———. "Of Other Spaces, Heterotopias." Translation of "Des espaces autres: Hétérotopies." Conférence au Cercle d'études architecturales, March 14, 1967. Published in *Architecture, Mouvement, Continuité* no. 5 (October 1984): 46–49. English translation, no author and no date, at www.foucault.info/documents/heterotopia/foucault.heterotopia.en.html (accessed September 20, 2013).

Friedman, Mildred. *Gehry Talks: Architecture and Process*. New York: Rizzoli International Publications Inc., 1999.

García Márquez, Gabriel. *Living to Tell the Tale*. Translation by Edith Grossman. New York: Knopf, 2003. Translation of *Vivir para contarla*.

———. *One Hundred Years of Solitude*. Translated by Gregory Rabassa. London: Penguin, 1973.

Gehry, Frank. "F.O.G. Talks on His Works: The lecture in Tokyo, 1985." *A+U: Architecture and Urbanism* 184 (January 1986): PAGE RANGE.

Gladwell, Malcolm. "The Terrazzo Jungle." *The New Yorker*. March 15, 2004.

Goldberger, Paul. "Three Works of Frank Gehry." *A+U: Architecture and Urbanism*. 184 (January 1986): PAGE RANGE.

Hardwick, M. Jeffrey. *Mall Maker: Victor Gruen, Architect of an American Dream*. Philadelphia: University of Pennsylvania Press, 2004.

Heidegger, Martin. "Building Dwelling Thinking." In *Basic Writings: From* Being and Time *(1927) to* The Task of Thinking *(1964)*, edited by David Farrell Krell, 323–39. New York: Harper & Row, 1977.

Hernández Martínez, Ascensión. *La Clonación Arquitectónica*. Madrid: Editorial Siruela, 2007.

Iñiguez, Manuel. *Tiempo y lugar en la obra de K. F. Schinkel y A. Aalto*. Euskal Herriko Unibertsiatearen argitalpen zerbitzua, 1997.

Jencks, Charles. "Frank O. Gehry: Creating Another Way." In *Frank O. Gehry: Individual Imagination and Cultural Conservatism*, edited by Charles Jencks, 6–7. London: Academy Editions, 1995.

———. "Individual Imagination and Cultural Conservatism: Royal Academy of Arts International Forum." In *Frank O. Gehry: Individual Imagination and Cultural Conservatism*, edited by Charles Jencks, 8–37. London: Academy Editions, 1995.

Kavafis, Kostandinos P. *Poema antologia*. "Ithaka." Iruña: Pamiela, 1995.

Kuleshov, Lev Vladimirovich. *Kuleshov on Film: Writings*. Edited by Ronald Levaco. Berkeley: University of California Press, 1975.

Leibniz, Gottfied. *New Essays on Human Understanding*. Translated and edited by Peter Remnant and Jonathan Bennet. Cambridge: Cambridge University Press, 1981.

Leibovitz, Aliel. "Lost in Translation: What Proust Taught me About Being Jewish." *Tablet Magazine*. November 18, 2008. Available at www.tabletmag.com/jewish-arts-and-culture/books/1004/lost-in-translation.

Lertxundi, Anjel. "Hitz beste," *Berria*, April 30, 2009.

Lévi-Strauss, Claude. *The Savage Mind*. Chicago: University of Chicago Press, 1968.

Marinetti, Filippo Tommaso. Founding and Manifesto of Futurism by F. T. Marinetti.: In *Documents of 20th Century Art: Futurist Manifestos*. Edited by Umbro Apollonio, translated by Robert Brain, R. W. Flint, J. C. Higgitt, and Caroline Tisdall, 19–24. New York: Viking Press, 1973. Originally published "Fondation et manifeste du Futurisme," in *Le Figaro*, February 20, 1909.

Marot, Sébastien. *Suburbanismo y el arte de la memoria*. Barcelona: Gustavo Gili, 2006.

Martienssen, R. D. *The Idea of Space in Greek Architecture*. Johannesburg: Wirwatersrand University Press, 1968.

Mastro, Ed, and Mike Schaadt. *San Pedro's Cabrillo Beach*. San Francisco: Arcadia Publishing, 2008.

———. *Cabrillo Beach Coastal Park*. San Francisco: Arcadia Publishing, 2009.

Mombiela, Edita. "Sobre la utilidad de nuestra Memoria en nuestra vida presente y nuestras esperanzas de futuro." *A parte rei: Revista de filosofía*, 19 zbk., 2002.

Moneo, Rafael. *Inquietud teórica y estrategia proyectual*. Barcelona: Actar, 2004.

———. "Reflexiones a propósito de dos salas de conciertos: Gehry versus Venturi (Walter Gropius Lecture. Graduate School of Design, Harvard University. 1990)." *El Croquis* no. 64 (1997): PAGE RANGE.

Moughtin, Cliff, with Peter Shirley. *Urban Design: Green Dimensions*. 2nd edition. Amsterdam: Elsevier, 2005.

Mutlow, John V. "Loyola Law School: Frank O. Gehry & Associates." *L.A. Architect*, January 1982.

Nietzsche, Friedrich. The Use and Abuse of History." In *Thoughts out of Season*, part 2, translated by Adrian Collins. Project Gutenberg edition, www.gutenberg.org/files/38226/38226-h/38226-h.htm, release date December 5, 2011.

Nottingham, Stephen. *Screening DNA: Exploring the Cinema-Genetics Interface*. The Internet Version. DNA Books, 1999.

Oteiza, Jorge. "Existe Dios al noroeste." In *Androcanto y sigo: Anotación final*. Iruña: Pamiela, 1990.

Padilla Aguilar, Maria Teresa. "La destrucción del recuerdo." *Odiseo: Rumbo al pasado* 1, (2001).

Pallasmaa, Juhani. *Los ojos de la piel*. Barcelona: Gustavo Gili, 2006.

Pastier, John. "Distillation or a Paradoxical City: Loyola Law School, Los Angeles." *Architecture*: the AIA journal, May 1985.

Pollan, Michael. *The Botany of Desire: A Plant's-Eye View of the World*. New York: Random House, 2001.

Porphyrios, Demetri. "Heterotopía: Un estudio sobre el orden en la obra de Aalto."In *Alvar Aalto*. Compiled by Victor Brosa. Barcelona: Ediciones del Serbal, 1998.

———. *Sources of Modern Eclecticism: Studies on Alvar Aalto*. New York: St. Martin's Press, 1982.

Proust, Marcel. *Swann's Way*. Volume 1. *In Search of Lost Time*. Translated by C. K. Scott Moncrieff and Terence Kilmartin, revised by D. J. Enright. New York: Modern Library, 1992.

———. *Time Regained.* Volume 7. *In Search of Lost Time.* Translated by Andreas Mayor. London: Chattus & Windus, 1970.

Rubino, Luciano. *Frank O. Gehry Special.* Rome: Kappa, 1984.

Russell, Bertrand. *The Analysis of Mind* [1921]. Project Gutenberg edition, www.gutenberg.org/files/2529/2529-h/2529-h.htm, last modified February 7, 2013.

Scalvini, Luisa. "Sghembo e trasparente : The Gehry intersection." *Domus* 631 (September1982): PAGE RANGE.

Schildt, Goran. *Alvar Aalto: Obra completa; Arquitectura, arte y diseño.* Barcelona: Gutavo Gili, 1996.

Soja, Edward W. "Inside Exopolis: Scenes from Orange County." In *Variations on a Theme Park: The New American City and the End of Public Space*, edited by Michael Sorkin, 94–122. New York: Hill & Wang/Noonday Press, 1992.

———. *Thirdspace. Journeys to Los Angeles and Other Real-and-Imagined Places.* Malden: Blachwell Publishing, 1996.

Sorkin, Michael. *Some Assembly Required.* Minneapolis / London: University of Minnesota Press, 2001.

St. John Wilson, Colin. *The Other Tradition of Modern Architecture: The Uncompleted Project.* London: Black Dog Publishing Ltd., 2007.

Stungo, Naomi. *Frank Gehry.* London: Carlton, 1999.

Treib, Marc. "Aalto's Nature." In *Alvar Aalto: Between Humanism and Materialism*, edited by Peter Reed, 47–67. New York: Museum of Modern Art, 1998.

Yates, Frances A. *The Art of Memory.* Madrid: Ediciones Siruela, 2005.

Walker Art Center. *The Architecture of Frank Gehry.* New York: Rizzoli, 1986.

Wilde, Oscar. "The Decay Of Lying." In *Intentions: Essays*, 1–56. New York: Brentanos, 1905.

Zabaleascoa, Anatxu. "Francisco Barba Corsini: Un arquitecto con más de una idea." *El País*, March, 12 2008.

———. "Hay que suprimir las teorías para empezar a pensar" (interview with Francisco Barba Corsini). *El País*, May 19, 2007.

Zaera, Alejandro. "Frank O. Gehry: Naturaleza muerta." *El Croquis*, 45 + 74/75, 2006.

Zardini, Mirko. *Frank O Gehry: America as Context.* Milan: Electa, 1994.

Zulaika, Joseba, and Anna Maria Guasch. *Learning from the Bilbao Guggenheim*. Reno: Center for Basque Studies, 2005.

Other Sources

Interview, Frank Gehry and Thomas Pritzker. Aspen, Colorado, July 3, 2009.

Dialogue between Frank Gehry and Paul Goldberger. Yale University Architecture Department, April 7, 2006

Index

www.ingramcontent.com/pod-product-compliance
Lightning Source LLC
LaVergne TN
LVHW091054080826
845145LV00002B/744